CompTIA
Security+™

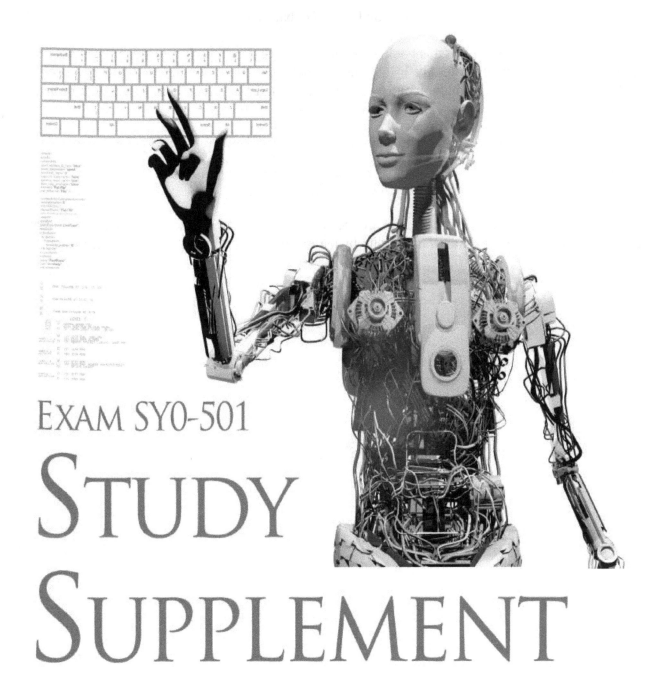

Exam SY0-501

Study
Supplement

Lowry Global Media LLC

Shue's, CompTIA Security+ Exam SY0-501, Study Supplement

Copyright © by Lowry Global Media LLC

ISBN: 978-1-945512-76-6

Contents

Introduction

I remember taking and passing the Security+ exam on my first try. It wasn't because I bought a 400+ page book and read it from cover to cover. It wasn't because I attended a week long instructor led crash course. It wasn't because I studied a book of exam questions and answers. It WAS because I had years of industry experience.

This book is not designed to walk you through all of the exam objectives chapter by chapter. It is designed to touch on a wide variety subjects to help jar your memory of all the stuff you are likely already familiar with. It is also designed to supplement another book you may have purchased to study, to give you some added exposure and experience.

Open source software is created by the community we belong to; IT professionals that want to do more and contribute. Just like open source software, this book has been created from open sources; a compilation of information for your benefit to help you pass the exam.

I would personally like wish you the best of luck on exam day. Get plenty of sleep, eat a good breakfast, and visualize your success. You can do it!!!

Enjoy,

Mark Schumacher
President
Lowry Global Media LLC

Information Security

Information security, sometimes shortened to InfoSec, is the practice of preventing unauthorized access, use, disclosure, disruption, modification, inspection, recording or destruction of information. It is a general term that can be used regardless of the form the data may take (e.g. electronic, physical).[1]

Information Security, Overview, IT Security

Sometimes referred to as computer security, information technology security (IT security) is information security applied to technology (most often some form of computer system). It is worthwhile to note that a computer does not necessarily mean a home desktop. A computer is any device with a processor and some memory. Such devices can range from non-networked standalone devices as simple as calculators, to networked mobile computing devices such as smartphones and tablet computers. IT security specialists are almost always found in any major enterprise/establishment due to the nature and value of the data within larger businesses. They are responsible for keeping all of the technology within the company secure from malicious cyber attacks that often attempt to breach into critical private information or gain control of the internal systems.

Information Security, Overview, Information Assurance

The act of providing trust of the information, that the Confidentiality, Integrity and Availability (CIA) of the information are not violated, e.g. ensuring that data is not lost when critical issues arise. These issues include, but are not limited to: natural disasters, computer/server malfunction or physical theft. Since most information is stored on computers in our modern era, information assurance is typically dealt with by IT security specialists. A common method of providing information assurance is to have an off-site backup of the data in case one of the mentioned issues arise.

Information Security, Threats

Information security threats come in many different forms. Some of the most common threats today are software attacks, theft of intellectual property, identity theft, theft of equipment or information, sabotage, and information extortion. Most people have experienced software attacks of some sort. Viruses,[2] worms, phishing attacks, and Trojan horses are a few common examples of software attacks. The theft of intellectual property has also been an extensive issue for many businesses in the IT field. Identity theft is the attempt to act as someone else usually to obtain that person's personal information or to take advantage of their access to vital information. Theft of equipment or information is becoming more prevalent today due to the fact that most devices today are mobile.[*citation needed*] Cell phones are prone to theft and have also become far more desirable as the amount of data capacity increases. Sabotage usually consists of the destruction of an organization's website in an attempt to cause loss of confidence on the part of its customers. Information extortion consists of theft of a company's property or information as an attempt to receive a payment in exchange for returning the information or property back to its owner, as with ransomware. There are many ways to help protect yourself from some of these attacks but one of the most functional precautions is user carefulness.

Governments, military, corporations, financial institutions, hospitals and private businesses amass a great deal of confidential information about their employees, customers, products, research and financial status. Most of this information is now collected, processed and stored on electronic computers and transmitted across networks to other computers.

Should confidential information about a business' customers or finances or new product line fall into the hands of a competitor or a black hat hacker, a business and its customers could suffer widespread, irreparable financial loss, as well as damage to the company's reputation. From a business perspective, information security must be balanced against cost; the Gordon-Loeb Model provides a mathematical economic approach for addressing this concern.[3]

For the individual, information security has a significant effect on privacy, which is viewed very differently in various cultures.

The field of information security has grown and evolved significantly in recent years. It offers many areas for specialization, including securing networks and allied infrastructure, securing applications and databases, security testing, information systems auditing, business continuity planning and digital forensics.

Information Security, Responses to Threats

Possible responses to a security threat or risk are:[4]

- Reduce/mitigate – implement safeguards and countermeasures to eliminate vulnerabilities or block threats
- Assign/transfer – place the cost of the threat onto another entity or organization such as purchasing insurance or outsourcing
- Accept – evaluate if cost of countermeasure outweighs the possible cost of loss due to threat
- Ignore/reject – not a valid or prudent due-care response

Information Security, History

Since the early days of communication, diplomats and military commanders understood that it was necessary to provide some mechanism to protect the confidentiality of correspondence and to have some means of detecting tampering. Julius Caesar is credited with the invention of the Caesar cipher c. 50 B.C., which was created in order to prevent his secret messages from being read should a message fall into the wrong hands, but for the most part protection was achieved through the application of procedural handling controls.[5][6] Sensitive information was marked up to indicate that it should be protected and transported by trusted persons, guarded and stored in a secure environment or strong box. As postal services expanded, governments created official organizations to intercept, decipher, read and reseal letters (e.g. the UK Secret Office and Deciphering Branch in 1653).

In the mid-19th century more complex classification systems were developed to allow governments to manage their information according to the degree of sensitivity. The British Government codified this, to some extent, with the publication of the Official Secrets Act in 1889. By the time of the First World War, multi-tier classification systems were used to communicate information to and from various fronts, which encouraged greater use of code making and breaking sections in diplomatic and military headquarters. In the United Kingdom this led to the creation of the Government Code and Cypher School in 1919. Encoding became more sophisticated between the wars as machines were employed to scramble and unscramble information. The volume of information shared by the Allied countries during the Second World War necessitated formal alignment of classification systems and procedural controls. An arcane range of markings evolved to indicate who could handle documents (usually officers rather than men) and where they should be stored as increasingly complex safes and storage facilities were developed. The Enigma Machine which was employed by the Germans to encrypt the data of warfare and successfully decrypted by Alan Turing can be regarded as a striking example of creating and using secured information. Procedures evolved to ensure documents were destroyed properly and it was the failure to follow these procedures which led to some of the greatest intelligence coups of the war (e.g. U-570).

The end of the 20th century and early years of the 21st century saw rapid advancements in telecommunications, computing hardware and software, and data encryption. The availability of smaller, more powerful and less expensive computing equipment made electronic data processing within the reach of small business and the home user. These computers quickly became interconnected through the Internet.

The rapid growth and widespread use of electronic data processing and electronic business conducted through the Internet, along with numerous occurrences of international terrorism, fueled the need for better methods of protecting the computers and the information they store, process and transmit. The academic disciplines of computer security and information assurance emerged along with numerous professional organizations – all sharing the common goals of ensuring the security and reliability of information systems.

Information Security, Definitions

Information Security Attributes: or qualities, i.e., Confidentiality, Integrity and Availability (CIA). Information Systems are composed in three main portions, hardware, software and communications with the purpose to help identify and apply information security industry standards, as mechanisms of protection and prevention, at three levels or layers: physical, personal and organizational. Essentially, procedures or policies are implemented to tell people (administrators, users and operators) how to use products to ensure information security within the organizations.

The definitions of InfoSec suggested in different sources are summarized below (adopted from).[7]

1. "Preservation of confidentiality, integrity and availability of information. Note: In addition, other properties, such as authenticity, accountability, non-repudiation and reliability can also be involved." (ISO/IEC 27000:2009)[8]
2. "The protection of information and information systems from unauthorized access, use, disclosure, disruption, modification, or destruction in order to provide confidentiality, integrity, and availability." (CNSS, 2010)[9]
3. "Ensures that only authorized users (confidentiality) have access to accurate and complete information (integrity) when required (availability)." (ISACA, 2008)[10]
4. "Information Security is the process of protecting the intellectual property of an organisation." (Pipkin, 2000)[11]
5. "...information security is a risk management discipline, whose job is to manage the cost of information risk to the business." (McDermott and Geer, 2001)[12]
6. "A well-informed sense of assurance that information risks and controls are in balance." (Anderson, J., 2003)[13]
7. "Information security is the protection of information and minimizes the risk of exposing information to unauthorized parties." (Venter and Eloff, 2003)[14]

8. "Information Security is a multidisciplinary area of study and professional activity which is concerned with the development and implementation of security mechanisms of all available types (technical, organizational, human-oriented and legal) in order to keep information in all its locations (within and outside the organization's perimeter) and, consequently, information systems, where information is created, processed, stored, transmitted and destroyed, free from threats.Threats to information and information systems may be categorized and a corresponding security goal may be defined for each category of threats. A set of security goals, identified as a result of a threat analysis, should be revised periodically to ensure its adequacy and conformance with the evolving environment. The currently relevant set of security goals may include: *confidentiality, integrity, availability, privacy, authenticity & trustworthiness, non-repudiation, accountability and auditability.*" (Cherdantseva and Hilton, 2013)[7]

Information Security, Employment

Information security is a stable and growing profession. Information security professionals are very stable in their employment; more than 80 percent had no change in employer or employment in the past year, and the number of professionals is projected to continuously grow more than 11 percent annually from 2014 to 2019.[15]

Information Security, Basic Principles, Key Concepts

The CIA triad of confidentiality, integrity, and availability is at the heart of information security.[16] (The members of the classic InfoSec triad — confidentiality, integrity and availability — are interchangeably referred to in the literature as security attributes, properties, security goals, fundamental aspects, information criteria, critical information characteristics and basic building blocks.) There is continuous debate about extending this classic trio.[7][*page needed*] Other principles such as Accountability have sometimes been proposed for addition – it has been pointed out that issues such as non-repudiation do not fit well within the three core concepts.[17]

In 1992 and revised in 2002, the OECD's *Guidelines for the Security of Information Systems and Networks*[18] proposed the nine generally accepted principles: awareness, responsibility, response, ethics, democracy, risk assessment, security design and implementation, security management, and reassessment. Building upon those, in 2004 the NIST's *Engineering Principles for Information Technology Security*[19] proposed 33 principles. From each of these derived guidelines and practices.

In 2002, Donn Parker proposed an alternative model for the classic CIA triad that he called the six atomic elements of information. The elements are confidentiality, possession, integrity, authenticity, availability, and utility. The merits of the Parkerian Hexad are a subject of debate amongst security professionals. [*citation needed*]

In 2011, The Open Group published the information security management standard O-ISM3.[20] This standard proposed an operational definition of the key concepts of security, with elements called "security objectives", related to access control (9), availability (3), data quality (1), compliance and technical (4). This model is not currently widely adopted.

Information Security, Basic Principles, Key Concepts, Confidentiality

In information security, confidentiality "is the property, that information is not made available or disclosed to unauthorized individuals, entities, or processes" (Excerpt ISO27000).

Information Security, Basic Principles, Key Concepts, Integrity

In information security, data integrity means maintaining and assuring the accuracy and completeness of data over its entire life-cycle.[21] This means that data cannot be modified in an unauthorized or undetected manner. This is not the same thing as referential integrity in databases, although it can be viewed as a special case of consistency as understood in the classic ACID model of transaction processing. Information security systems typically provide message integrity in addition to data confidentiality.

Information Security, Basic Principles, Key Concepts, Availability

For any information system to serve its purpose, the information must be available when it is needed. This means that the computing systems used to store and process the information, the security controls used to protect it, and the communication channels used to access it must be functioning correctly. High availability systems aim to remain available at all times, preventing service disruptions due to power outages, hardware failures, and system upgrades. Ensuring availability also involves preventing denial-of-service attacks, such as a flood of incoming messages to the target system essentially forcing it to shut down.[22]

Information Security, Basic Principles, Key Concepts, Non-repudiation

In law, non-repudiation implies one's intention to fulfill their obligations to a contract. It also implies that one party of a transaction cannot deny having received a transaction nor can the other party deny having sent a transaction.

It is important to note that while technology such as cryptographic systems can assist in non-repudiation efforts, the concept is at its core a legal concept transcending the realm of technology. It is not, for instance, sufficient to show that the message matches a digital signature signed with the sender's private key, and thus only the sender could have sent the message and nobody else could have altered it in transit (data integrity). The alleged sender could in return demonstrate that the digital signature algorithm is vulnerable or flawed, or allege or prove that his signing key has been compromised. The fault for these violations may or may not lie with the sender himself, and such assertions may or may not relieve the sender of liability, but the assertion would invalidate the claim that the signature necessarily proves authenticity and integrity; and, therefore, the sender may repudiate the message (because authenticity and integrity are pre-requisites for non-repudiation).

Information Security, Risk Management

The *Certified Information Systems Auditor (CISA) Review Manual 2006* provides the following definition of risk management: "Risk management is the process of identifying vulnerabilities and threats to the information resources used by an organization in achieving business objectives, and deciding what countermeasures, if any, to take in reducing risk to an acceptable level, based on the value of the information resource to the organization."[23]

There are two things in this definition that may need some clarification. First, the *process* of risk management is an ongoing, iterative process. It must be repeated indefinitely. The business environment is constantly changing and new threats and vulnerabilities emerge every day. Second, the choice of countermeasures (controls) used to manage risks must strike a balance between productivity, cost, effectiveness of the countermeasure, and the value of the informational asset being protected.

Risk analysis and risk evaluation processes have their limitations since, when security incidents occur, they emerge in a context, and their rarity and even their uniqueness give rise to unpredictable threats. The analysis of these phenomena which are characterized by breakdowns, surprises and side-effects, requires a theoretical approach which is able to examine and interpret subjectively the detail of each incident.[24]

Risk is the likelihood that something bad will happen that causes harm to an informational asset (or the loss of the asset). A vulnerability is a weakness that could be used to endanger or cause harm to an informational asset. A threat is anything (man-made or act of nature) that has the potential to cause harm.

The likelihood that a threat will use a vulnerability to cause harm creates a risk. When a threat does use a vulnerability to inflict harm, it has an impact. In the context of information security, the impact is a loss of availability, integrity, and confidentiality, and possibly other losses (lost income, loss of life, loss of real property). It should be pointed out that it is not possible to identify all risks, nor is it possible to eliminate all risk. The remaining risk is called "residual risk".

A risk assessment is carried out by a team of people who have knowledge of specific areas of the business. Membership of the team may vary over time as different parts of the business are assessed. The assessment may use a subjective qualitative analysis based on informed opinion, or where reliable dollar figures and historical information is available, the analysis may use quantitative analysis.

The research has shown that the most vulnerable point in most information systems is the human user, operator, designer, or other human.[25] The ISO/IEC 27002:2005 Code of practice for information security management recommends the following be examined during a risk assessment:

- security policy,
- organization of information security,
- asset management,
- human resources security,
- physical and environmental security,
- communications and operations management,
- access control,
- information systems acquisition, development and maintenance,
- information security incident management,
- business continuity management, and
- regulatory compliance.

In broad terms, the risk management process consists of:

1. Identification of assets and estimating their value. Include: people, buildings, hardware, software, data (electronic, print, other), supplies.
2. Conduct a threat assessment. Include: Acts of nature, acts of war, accidents, malicious acts originating from inside or outside the organization.
3. Conduct a vulnerability assessment, and for each vulnerability, calculate the probability that it will be exploited. Evaluate policies, procedures, standards, training, physical security, quality control, technical security.
4. Calculate the impact that each threat would have on each asset. Use qualitative analysis or quantitative analysis.
5. Identify, select and implement appropriate controls. Provide a proportional response. Consider productivity, cost effectiveness, and value of the asset.
6. Evaluate the effectiveness of the control measures. Ensure the controls provide the required cost effective protection without discernible loss of productivity.

For any given risk, management can choose to accept the risk based upon the relative low value of the asset, the relative low frequency of occurrence, and the relative low impact on the business. Or, leadership may choose to mitigate the risk by selecting and implementing appropriate control measures to reduce the risk. In some cases, the risk can be transferred to another business by buying insurance or outsourcing to another business.[26] The reality of some risks may be disputed. In such cases leadership may choose to deny the risk.

Information Security, Security Controls

Selecting proper controls and implementing those will initially help an organization to bring down risk to acceptable levels. Control selection should follow and should be based on the risk assessment. Controls can vary in nature but fundamentally they are ways of protecting the confidentiality, integrity or availability of information. ISO/IEC 27001:2005 has defined 133 controls in different areas, but this is not exhaustive. Organizations can implement additional controls according to requirement of the organization. ISO 27001:2013 has cut down the number of controls to 113. From 08.11.2013 the technical standard of information security in place is: ABNT NBR ISO/IEC 27002:2013.[27]

Information Security, Security Controls, Administrative

Administrative controls (also called procedural controls) consist of approved written policies, procedures, standards and guidelines. Administrative controls form the framework for running the business and managing people. They inform people on how the business is to be run and how day-to-day operations are to be conducted. Laws and regulations created by government bodies are also a type of administrative control because they inform the business. Some industry sectors have policies, procedures, standards and guidelines that must be followed – the Payment Card Industry Data Security Standard (PCI DSS) required by Visa and MasterCard is such an example. Other examples of administrative controls include the corporate security policy, password policy, hiring policies, and disciplinary policies.

Administrative controls form the basis for the selection and implementation of logical and physical controls. Logical and physical controls are manifestations of administrative controls. Administrative controls are of paramount importance.

Information Security, Security Controls, Logical

Logical controls (also called technical controls) use software and data to monitor and control access to information and computing systems. For example: passwords, network and host-based firewalls, network intrusion detection systems, access control lists, and data encryption are logical controls.

An important logical control that is frequently overlooked is the principle of least privilege. The principle of least privilege requires that an individual, program or system process is not granted any more access privileges than are necessary to perform the task. A blatant example of the failure to adhere to the principle of least privilege is logging into Windows as user Administrator to read email and surf the web. Violations of this principle can also occur when an individual collects additional access privileges over time. This happens when employees' job duties change, or they are promoted to a new position, or they transfer to another department. The access privileges required by their new duties are frequently added onto their already existing access privileges which may no longer be necessary or appropriate.

Information Security, Security Controls, Physical

Physical controls monitor and control the environment of the work place and computing facilities. They also monitor and control access to and from such facilities. For example: doors, locks, heating and air conditioning, smoke and fire alarms, fire suppression systems, cameras, barricades, fencing, security guards, cable locks, etc. Separating the network and workplace into functional areas are also physical controls.

An important physical control that is frequently overlooked is the separation of duties, which ensures that an individual can not complete a critical task by himself. For example: an employee who submits a request for reimbursement should not also be able to authorize payment or print the check. An applications programmer should not also be the server administrator or the database administrator – these roles and responsibilities must be separated from one another.[28]

Information Security, Defense in Depth

Information security must protect information throughout the life span of the information, from the initial creation of the information on through to the final disposal of the information. The information must be protected while in motion and while at rest. During its lifetime, information may pass through many different information processing systems and through many different parts of information processing systems. There are many different ways the information and information systems can be threatened. To fully protect the information during its lifetime, each component of the information processing system must have its own protection mechanisms. The building up, layering on and overlapping of security measures is called defense in depth. In contrast to a metal chain, which is famously only as strong as its weakest link, the defense-in-depth aims at a structure where, should one defensive measure fail, other measures will continue to provide protection.

Recall the earlier discussion about administrative controls, logical controls, and physical controls. The three types of controls can be used to form the basis upon which to build a defense-in-depth strategy. With this approach, defense-in-depth can be conceptualized as three distinct layers or planes laid one on top of the other. Additional insight into defense-in- depth can be gained by thinking of it as forming the layers of an onion, with data at the core of the onion, people the next outer layer of the onion, and network security, host-based security and application security forming the outermost layers of the onion. Both perspectives are equally valid and each provides valuable insight into the implementation of a good defense-in-depth strategy.

Information Security, Access Control

Access to protected information must be restricted to people who are authorized to access the information. The computer programs, and in many cases the computers that process the information, must also be authorized. This requires that mechanisms be in place to control the access to protected information. The sophistication of the access control mechanisms should be in parity with the value of the information being protected – the more sensitive or valuable the information the stronger the control mechanisms need to be. The foundation on which access control mechanisms are built start with identification and authentication.

Access control is generally considered in three steps: Identification, Authentication, and Authorization.

Information Security, Access Control, Identification

Identification is an assertion of who someone is or what something is. If a person makes the statement "Hello, my name is John Doe" they are making a claim of who they are. However, their claim may or may not be true. Before John Doe can be granted access to protected information it will be necessary to verify that the person claiming to be John Doe really is John Doe. Typically the claim is in the form of a username. By entering that username you are claiming "I am the person the username belongs to".

Information Security, Access Control, Authentication

Authentication is the act of verifying a claim of identity. When John Doe goes into a bank to make a withdrawal, he tells the bank teller he is John Doe—a claim of identity. The bank teller asks to see a photo ID, so he hands the teller his driver's license. The bank teller checks the license to make sure it has John Doe printed on it and compares the photograph on the license against the person claiming to be John Doe. If the photo and name match the person, then the teller has authenticated that John Doe is who he claimed to be. Similarly by entering the correct password, the user is providing evidence that he/she is the person the username belongs to.

There are three different types of information that can be used for authentication:

- Something you know: things such as a PIN, a password, or your mother's maiden name.
- Something you have: a driver's license or a magnetic swipe card.
- Something you are: biometrics, including palm prints, fingerprints, voice prints and retina (eye) scans.

Strong authentication requires providing more than one type of authentication information (two-factor authentication). The username is the most common form of identification on computer systems today and the password is the most common form of authentication. Usernames and passwords have served their purpose but in our modern world they are no longer adequate.[*citation needed*] Usernames and passwords are slowly being replaced with more sophisticated authentication mechanisms.

Information Security, Access Control, Authorization

After a person, program or computer has successfully been identified and authenticated then it must be determined what informational resources they are permitted to access and what actions they will be allowed to perform (run, view, create, delete, or change). This is called authorization. Authorization to access information and other computing services begins with administrative policies and procedures. The policies prescribe what information and computing services can be accessed, by whom, and under what conditions. The access control mechanisms are then configured to enforce these policies. Different computing systems are equipped with different kinds of access control mechanisms—some may even offer a choice of different access control mechanisms. The access control mechanism a system offers will be based upon one of three approaches to access control or it may be derived from a combination of the three approaches.

The non-discretionary approach consolidates all access control under a centralized administration. The access to information and other resources is usually based on the individuals function (role) in the organization or the tasks the individual must perform. The discretionary approach gives the creator or owner of the information resource the ability to control access to those resources. In the Mandatory access control approach, access is granted or denied basing upon the security classification assigned to the information resource.

Examples of common access control mechanisms in use today include role-based access control available in many advanced database management systems—simple file permissions provided in the UNIX and Windows operating systems, Group Policy Objects provided in Windows network systems, Kerberos, RADIUS, TACACS, and the simple access lists used in many firewalls and routers.

To be effective, policies and other security controls must be enforceable and upheld. Effective policies ensure that people are held accountable for their actions. All failed and successful authentication attempts must be logged, and all access to information must leave some type of audit trail.[*citation needed*]

Also, need-to-know principle needs to be in effect when talking about access control. Need-to-know principle gives access rights to a person to perform their job functions. This principle is used in the government, when dealing with difference clearances. Even though two employees in different departments have a top-secret clearance, they must have a need-to-know in order for information to be exchanged. Within the need-to-know principle, network administrators grant the employee least amount privileges to prevent employees access and doing more than what they are supposed to. Need-to-know helps to enforce the confidentiality-integrity-availability (C-I-A) triad. Need-to-know directly impacts the confidential area of the triad.

Information Security, Cryptography

Information security uses cryptography to transform usable information into a form that renders it unusable by anyone other than an authorized user; this process is called encryption. Information that has been encrypted (rendered unusable) can be transformed back into its original usable form by an authorized user, who possesses the cryptographic key, through the process of decryption. Cryptography is used in information security to protect information from unauthorized or accidental disclosure while the information is in transit (either electronically or physically) and while information is in storage.

Cryptography provides information security with other useful applications as well including improved authentication methods, message digests, digital signatures, non-repudiation, and encrypted network communications. Older less secure applications such as telnet and ftp are slowly being replaced with more secure applications such as ssh that use encrypted network communications. Wireless communications can be encrypted using protocols such as WPA/WPA2 or the older (and less secure) WEP. Wired communications (such as ITU-T G.hn) are secured using AES for encryption and X.1035 for authentication and key exchange. Software applications such as GnuPG or PGP can be used to encrypt data files and Email.

Cryptography can introduce security problems when it is not implemented correctly. Cryptographic solutions need to be implemented using industry accepted solutions that have undergone rigorous peer review by independent experts in cryptography. The length and strength of the encryption key is also an important consideration. A key that is weak or too short will produce weak encryption. The keys used for encryption and decryption must be protected with the same degree of rigor as any other confidential information. They must be protected from unauthorized disclosure and destruction and they must be available when needed. Public key infrastructure (PKI) solutions address many of the problems that surround key management.

Internet Security

Internet security is a branch of computer security specifically related to the Internet, often involving browser security but also network security on a more general level as it applies to other applications or operating systems on a whole. Its objective is to establish rules and measures to use against attacks over the Internet.[1] The Internet represents an insecure channel for exchanging information leading to a high risk of intrusion or fraud, such as phishing.[2] Different methods have been used to protect the transfer of data, including encryption and from-the-ground-up engineering.[3]

Internet Security, Threats, Malicious Software

A computer user can be tricked or forced into downloading software onto a computer that is of malicious intent. Such software comes in many forms, such as viruses, Trojan horses, spyware, and worms.

- Malware, short for malicious software, is any software used to disrupt computer operation, gather sensitive information, or gain access to private computer systems. Malware is defined by its malicious intent, acting against the requirements of the computer user, and does not include software that causes unintentional harm due to some deficiency. The term badware is sometimes used, and applied to both true (malicious) malware and unintentionally harmful software.
- A botnet is a network of zombie computers that have been taken over by a robot or bot that performs large-scale malicious acts for the creator of the botnet.
- Computer Viruses are programs that can replicate their structures or effects by infecting other files or structures on a computer. The common use of a virus is to take over a computer to steal data.
- Computer worms are programs that can replicate themselves throughout a computer network, performing malicious tasks throughout.
- Ransomware is a type of malware which restricts access to the computer system that it infects, and

demands a ransom paid to the creator(s) of the malware in order for the restriction to be removed.

- Scareware is scam software with malicious payloads, usually of limited or no benefit, that are sold to consumers via certain unethical marketing practices. The selling approach uses social engineering to cause shock, anxiety, or the perception of a threat, generally directed at an unsuspecting user.
- Spyware refers to programs that surreptitiously monitor activity on a computer system and report that information to others without the user's consent.
- A Trojan horse, commonly known as a *Trojan*, is a general term for malicious software that pretends to be harmless, so that a user willingly allows it to be downloaded onto the computer.
- KeyLogger, Keystroke logging, often referred to as keylogging or keyboard capturing, is the action of recording (logging) the keys struck on a keyboard

Internet Security, Threats, Denial-of-service Attacks

A denial-of-service attack (DoS attack) or distributed denial-of-service attack (DDoS attack) is an attempt to make a computer resource unavailable to its intended users. Although the means to carry out, motives for, and targets of a DoS attack may vary, it generally consists of the concerted efforts to prevent an Internet site or service from functioning efficiently or at all, temporarily or indefinitely. According to businesses who participated in an international business security survey, 25% of respondents experienced a DoS attack in 2007 and 16.8% experienced one in 2010.[4]

Internet Security, Threats, Phishing

Phishing occurs when the attacker pretends to be a trustworthy entity, either via email or web page. Victims are directed to fake web pages, which are dressed to look legitimate, via spoof emails, instant messenger/social media or other avenues. Often tactics such as email spoofing are used to make emails appear to be from legitimate senders, or long complex subdomains hide the real website host.[5][6] Insurance group RSA said that phishing accounted for worldwide losses of $1.5 billion in 2012.[7]

Internet Security, Threats, Application Vulnerabilities

Applications used to access Internet resources may contain security vulnerabilities such as memory safety bugs or flawed authentication checks. The most severe of these bugs can give network attackers full control over the computer. Most security applications and suites are incapable of adequate defense against these kinds of attacks.[8][9]

Internet Security, Remedies, Network Layer Security

TCP/IP protocols may be secured with cryptographic methods and security protocols. These protocols include Secure Sockets Layer (SSL), succeeded by Transport Layer Security (TLS) for web traffic, Pretty Good Privacy (PGP) for email, and IPsec for the network layer security.

Internet Security, Remedies, Internet Protocol Security (IPsec)

IPsec is designed to protect TCP/IP communication in a secure manner. It is a set of security extensions developed by the Internet Task Force (IETF). It provides security and authentication at the IP layer by transforming data using encryption. Two main types of transformation that form the basis of IPsec: the Authentication Header (AH) and ESP. These two protocols provide data integrity, data origin authentication, and anti-replay service. These protocols can be used alone or in combination to provide the desired set of security services for the Internet Protocol (IP) layer.

The basic components of the IPsec security architecture are described in terms of the following functionalities:

- Security protocols for AH and ESP
- Security association for policy management and traffic processing
- Manual and automatic key management for the Internet key exchange (IKE)
- Algorithms for authentication and encryption

The set of security services provided at the IP layer includes access control, data origin integrity, protection against replays, and confidentiality. The algorithm allows these sets to work independently without affecting other parts of the implementation. The IPsec implementation is operated in a host or security gateway environment giving protection to IP traffic.

Internet Security, Remedies, Security Token

Some online sites offer customers the ability to use a six-digit code which randomly changes every 30–60 seconds on a security token. The keys on the security token have built in mathematical computations and manipulate numbers based on the current time built into the device. This means that every thirty seconds there is only a certain array of numbers possible which would be correct to validate access to the online account. The website that the user is logging into would be made aware of that device's serial number and would know the computation and correct time built into the device to verify that the number given is indeed one of the handful of six-digit numbers that works in that given 30-60 second cycle. After 30–60 seconds the device will present a new random six-digit number which can log into the website.[10]

Internet Security, Remedies, Electronic Mail Security, Background

Email messages are composed, delivered, and stored in a multiple step process, which starts with the message's composition. When the user finishes composing the message and sends it, the message is transformed into a standard format: an RFC 2822 formatted message. Afterwards, the message can be transmitted. Using a network connection, the mail client, referred to as a mail user agent (MUA), connects to a mail transfer agent (MTA) operating on the mail server. The mail client then provides the sender's identity to the server. Next, using the mail server commands, the client sends the recipient list to the mail server. The client then supplies the message. Once the mail server receives and processes the message, several events occur: recipient server identification, connection establishment, and message transmission. Using Domain Name System (DNS) services, the sender's mail server determines the mail server(s) for the recipient(s). Then, the server opens up a connection(s) to the recipient mail server(s) and sends the message employing a process similar to that used by the originating client, delivering the message to the recipient(s).

Internet Security, Remedies, Electronic Mail Security, Pretty Good Privacy (PGP)

Pretty Good Privacy provides confidentiality by encrypting messages to be transmitted or data files to be stored using an encryption algorithm such as Triple DES or CAST-128. Email messages can be protected by using cryptography in various ways, such as the following:

- Signing an email message to ensure its integrity and confirm the identity of its sender.
- Encrypting the body of an email message to ensure its confidentiality.
- Encrypting the communications between mail servers to protect the confidentiality of both message body and message header.

The first two methods, message signing and message body encryption, are often used together; however, encrypting the transmissions between mail servers is typically used only when two organizations want to protect emails regularly sent between each other. For example, the organizations could establish a virtual private network (VPN) to encrypt the communications between their mail servers over the Internet.[11] Unlike methods that can only encrypt a message body, a VPN can encrypt entire messages, including email header information such as senders, recipients, and subjects. In some cases, organizations may need to protect header information. However, a VPN solution alone cannot provide a message signing mechanism, nor can it provide protection for email messages along the entire route from sender to recipient.

Internet Security, Remedies, Electronic Mail Security, Multipurpose Internet Mail Extensions (MIME)

MIME transforms non-ASCII data at the sender's site to Network Virtual Terminal (NVT) ASCII data and delivers it to client's Simple Mail Transfer Protocol (SMTP) to be sent through the Internet.[12] The server SMTP at the receiver's side receives the NVT ASCII data and delivers it to MIME to be transformed back to the original non-ASCII data.

Internet Security, Remedies, Electronic Mail Security, Message Authentication Code

A Message authentication code (MAC) is a cryptography method that uses a secret key to encrypt a message. This method outputs a MAC value that can be decrypted by the receiver, using the same secret key used by the sender. The Message Authentication Code protects both a message's data integrity as well as its authenticity.[13]

Internet Security, Firewalls

A computer firewall controls access between networks. It generally consists of gateways and filters which vary from one firewall to another. Firewalls also screen network traffic and are able to block traffic that is dangerous. Firewalls act as the intermediate server between SMTP and Hypertext Transfer Protocol (HTTP) connections.[14]

Internet Security, Firewalls, Role of Firewalls in Web Security

Firewalls impose restrictions on incoming and outgoing Network packets to and from private networks. Incoming or outgoing traffic must pass through the firewall; only authorized traffic is allowed to pass through it. Firewalls create checkpoints between an internal private network and the public Internet, also known as *choke points* (borrowed from the identical military term of a combat limiting geographical feature). Firewalls can create choke points based on IP source and TCP port number. They can also serve as the platform for IPsec. Using tunnel mode capability, firewall can be used to implement VPNs. Firewalls can also limit network exposure by hiding the internal network system and information from the public Internet.

Internet Security, Firewalls, Types of Firewall, Packet Filter

A packet filter is a first generation firewall that processes network traffic on a packet-by-packet basis. Its main job is to filter traffic from a remote IP host, so a router is needed to connect the internal network to the Internet. The router is known as a screening router, which screens packets leaving and entering the network.

Internet Security, Firewalls, Types of Firewall, Stateful Packet Inspection

In a stateful firewall the circuit-level gateway is a proxy server that operates at the network level of an Open Systems Interconnection (OSI) model and statically defines what traffic will be allowed. Circuit proxies will forward Network packets (formatted unit of data) containing a given port number, if the port is permitted by the algorithm. The main advantage of a proxy server is its ability to provide Network Address Translation (NAT), which can hide the user's IP address from the Internet, effectively protecting all internal information from the Internet.

Internet Security, Firewalls, Types of Firewall, Application-level Gateway

An application-level firewall is a third generation firewall where a proxy server operates at the very top of the OSI model, the IP suite application level. A network packet is forwarded only if a connection is established using a known protocol. Application-level gateways are notable for analyzing entire messages rather than individual packets of data when the data are being sent or received.

Internet Security, Browser Security

Web browser statistics tend to affect the amount a Web browser is exploited. For example, Internet Explorer 6, which used to own a majority of the Web browser market share,[15] is considered extremely insecure[16] because vulnerabilities were exploited due to its former popularity. Since browser choice is now more evenly distributed (Internet Explorer at 28.5%, Firefox at 18.4%, Google Chrome at 40.8%, and so on),[15] vulnerabilities are exploited in many different browsers.[17][18][19]

Internet Security, Internet Security Products, Antivirus

Antivirus software and Internet security programs can protect a programmable device from attack by detecting and eliminating viruses; Antivirus software was mainly shareware in the early years of the Internet,[*when?*] but there are now[*when?*] several free security applications on the Internet to choose from for all platforms.[20]

Internet Security, Internet Security Products, Password Managers

A password manager is a software application that helps a user store and organize passwords. Password managers usually store passwords encrypted, requiring the user to create a master password; a single, ideally very strong password which grants the user access to their entire password database.[21]

Internet Security, Internet Security Products, Security Suites

So called *security suites* were first offered for sale in 2003 (McAfee) and contain a suite of firewalls, anti-virus, anti-spyware and more.[22] They also offer theft protection, portable storage device safety check, private Internet browsing, cloud anti-spam, a file shredder or make security-related decisions (answering popup windows) and several were free of charge.[23]

Computer Security

Computer security, also known as cyber security or IT security, is the protection of computer systems from the theft or damage to their hardware, software or information, as well as from disruption or misdirection of the services they provide.[1]

Cyber security includes controlling physical access to the hardware, as well as protecting against harm that may come via network access, data and code injection.[2] Also, due to malpractice by operators, whether intentional, accidental, IT security is susceptible to being tricked into deviating from secure procedures through various methods.[3]

The field is of growing importance due to the increasing reliance on computer systems and the Internet,[4] wireless networks such as Bluetooth and Wi-Fi, and the growth of "smart" devices, including smartphones, televisions and tiny devices as part of the Internet of Things.

Computer Security, Vulnerabilities and Attacks

A vulnerability is a weakness in design, implementation, operation or internal control. As they are discovered many vulnerabilities are documented in the Common Vulnerabilities and Exposures (CVE) database.

An *exploitable* vulnerability is one for which at least one working attack or "exploit" exists.[5] Vulnerabilities are often hunted or exploited with the aid of automated tools.

To secure a computer system, it is important to understand the attacks that can be made against it, and these threats can typically be classified into one of the categories below:

Computer Security, Vulnerabilities and Attacks, Backdoor

A backdoor in a computer system, a cryptosystem or an algorithm, is any secret method of bypassing normal authentication or security controls. They may exist for a number of reasons, including by original design or from poor configuration. They may have been added by an authorized party to allow some legitimate access, or by an attacker for malicious reasons; but regardless of the motives for their existence, they create a vulnerability.

Computer Security, Vulnerabilities and Attacks, Denial-of-service Attack

Denial of service attacks (DoS) are designed to make a machine or network resource unavailable to its intended users.[6] Attackers can deny service to individual victims, such as by deliberately entering a wrong password enough consecutive times to cause the victim account to be locked, or they may overload the capabilities of a machine or network and block all users at once. While a network attack from a single IP address can be blocked by adding a new firewall rule, many forms of Distributed denial of service (DDoS) attacks are possible, where the attack comes from a large number of points – and defending is much more difficult. Such attacks can originate from the zombie computers of a botnet, but a range of other techniques are possible including reflection and amplification attacks, where innocent systems are fooled into sending traffic to the victim.

Computer Security, Vulnerabilities and Attacks, Direct-access Attacks

An unauthorized user gaining physical access to a computer is most likely able to directly copy data from it. They may also compromise security by making operating system modifications, installing software worms, keyloggers, covert listening devices or using wireless mice.[7] Even when the system is protected by standard security measures, these may be able to be by-passed by booting another operating system or tool from a CD-ROM or other bootable media. Disk encryption and Trusted Platform Module are designed to prevent these attacks.

Computer Security, Vulnerabilities and Attacks, Eavesdropping

Eavesdropping is the act of surreptitiously listening to a private conversation, typically between hosts on a network. For instance, programs such as Carnivore and NarusInSight have been used by the FBI and NSA to eavesdrop on the systems of internet service providers. Even machines that operate as a closed system (i.e., with no contact to the outside world) can be eavesdropped upon via monitoring the faint electro-magnetic transmissions generated by the hardware; TEMPEST is a specification by the NSA referring to these attacks.

Computer Security, Vulnerabilities and Attacks, Tampering

Tampering describes a malicious modification of products. So-called "Evil Maid" attacks and security services planting of surveillance capability into routers[9] are examples.

Computer Security, Vulnerabilities and Attacks, Privilege Escalation

Privilege escalation describes a situation where an attacker with some level of restricted access is able to, without authorization, elevate their privileges or access level. For example, a standard computer user may be able to fool the system into giving them access to restricted data; or even to "become root" and have full unrestricted access to a system.

Computer Security, Vulnerabilities and Attacks, Phishing

Phishing is the attempt to acquire sensitive information such as usernames, passwords, and credit card details directly from users.[10] Phishing is typically carried out by email spoofing or instant messaging, and it often directs users to enter details at a fake website whose look and feel are almost identical to the legitimate one. Preying on a victim's trust, phishing can be classified as a form of social engineering.

Computer Security, Vulnerabilities and Attacks, Clickjacking

Clickjacking, also known as "UI redress attack" or "User Interface redress attack", is a malicious technique in which an attacker tricks a user into clicking on a button or link on another webpage while the user intended to click on the top level page. This is done using multiple transparent or opaque layers. The attacker is basically "hijacking" the clicks meant for the top level page and routing them to some other irrelevant page, most likely owned by someone else. A similar technique can be used to hijack keystrokes. Carefully drafting a combination of stylesheets, iframes, buttons and text boxes, a user can be led into believing that they are typing the password or other information on some authentic webpage while it is being channeled into an invisible frame controlled by the attacker.

Computer Security, Vulnerabilities and Attacks, Social Engineering

Social engineering aims to convince a user to disclose secrets such as passwords, card numbers, etc. by, for example, impersonating a bank, a contractor, or a customer.[11]

A common scam involves fake CEO emails sent to accounting and finance departments. In early 2016, the FBI reported that the scam has cost US businesses more than $2bn in about two years.[12]

In May 2016, the Milwaukee Bucks NBA team was the victim of this type of cyber scam with a perpetrator impersonating the team's president Peter Feigin, resulting in the handover of all the team's employees' 2015 W-2 tax forms.[13]

Computer Security, Information Security Culture

Employee behavior can have a big impact on information security in organizations. Cultural concepts can help different segments of the organization work effectively or work against effectiveness towards information security within an organization."Exploring the Relationship between Organizational Culture and Information Security Culture" provides the following definition of information security culture: "ISC is the totality of patterns of behavior in an organization that contribute to the protection of information of all kinds."[14]

Andersson and Reimers (2014) found that employees often do not see themselves as part of the organization Information Security "effort" and often take actions that ignore organizational Information Security best interests.[15] Research shows Information security culture needs to be improved continuously. In "Information Security Culture from Analysis to Change", authors commented, "It's a never ending process, a cycle of evaluation and change or maintenance." To manage the information security culture, five steps should be taken: Pre-evaluation, strategic planning, operative planning, implementation, and post-evaluation.[16]

- Pre-Evaluation: to identify the awareness of information security within employees and to analyze the current security policy.
- Strategic Planning: to come up with a better awareness program, clear targets need to be set. Clustering people is helpful to achieve it.
- Operative Planning: a good security culture can be established based on internal communication, management-buy-in, and security awareness and a training program.[16]
- Implementation: four stages should be used to implement the information security culture. They are commitment of the management, communication with organizational members, courses for all organizational members, and commitment of the employees.[16]

Computer Security, Computer Protection (countermeasures)

In computer security a countermeasure is an action, device, procedure, or technique that reduces a threat, a vulnerability, or an attack by eliminating or preventing it, by minimizing the harm it can cause, or by discovering and reporting it so that corrective action can be taken.[83][84][85]

Some common countermeasures are listed in the following sections:

Computer Security, Computer Protection (countermeasures), Security by Design

Security by design, or alternately secure by design, means that the software has been designed from the ground up to be secure. In this case, security is considered as a main feature.

Some of the techniques in this approach include:

- The principle of least privilege, where each part of the system has only the privileges that are needed for its function. That way even if an attacker gains access to that part, they have only limited access to the whole system.
- Automated theorem proving to prove the correctness of crucial software subsystems.
- Code reviews and unit testing, approaches to make modules more secure where formal correctness proofs are not possible.
- Defense in depth, where the design is such that more than one subsystem needs to be violated to compromise the integrity of the system and the information it holds.
- Default secure settings, and design to "fail secure" rather than "fail insecure" (see fail-safe for the equivalent in safety engineering). Ideally, a secure system should require a deliberate, conscious, knowledgeable and free decision on the part of legitimate authorities in order to make it insecure.
- Audit trails tracking system activity, so that when a security breach occurs, the mechanism and extent of the breach can be determined. Storing audit trails remotely, where they can only be appended to, can keep intruders from covering their tracks.
- Full disclosure of all vulnerabilities, to ensure that the "window of vulnerability" is kept as short as possible when bugs are discovered.

Computer Security, Computer Protection (countermeasures), Security Architecture

The Open Security Architecture organization defines IT security architecture as "the design artifacts that describe how the security controls (security countermeasures) are positioned, and how they relate to the overall information technology architecture. These controls serve the purpose to maintain the system's quality attributes: confidentiality, integrity, availability, accountability and assurance services".[86]

Techopedia defines security architecture as "a unified security design that addresses the necessities and potential risks involved in a certain scenario or environment. It also specifies when and where to apply security controls. The design process is generally reproducible." The key attributes of security architecture are:[87]

- the relationship of different components and how they depend on each other.
- the determination of controls based on risk assessment, good practice, finances, and legal matters.
- the standardization of controls.

Computer Security, Computer Protection (countermeasures), Security Measures

A state of computer "security" is the conceptual ideal, attained by the use of the three processes: threat prevention, detection, and response. These processes are based on various policies and system components, which include the following:

- User account access controls and cryptography can protect systems files and data, respectively.
- Firewalls are by far the most common prevention systems from a network security perspective as they can (if properly configured) shield access to internal network services, and block certain kinds of attacks through packet filtering. Firewalls can be both hardware- or software-based.

- Intrusion Detection System (IDS) products are designed to detect network attacks in-progress and assist in post-attack forensics, while audit trails and logs serve a similar function for individual systems.
- "Response" is necessarily defined by the assessed security requirements of an individual system and may cover the range from simple upgrade of protections to notification of legal authorities, counter-attacks, and the like. In some special cases, a complete destruction of the compromised system is favored, as it may happen that not all the compromised resources are detected.

Today, computer security comprises mainly "preventive" measures, like firewalls or an exit procedure. A firewall can be defined as a way of filtering network data between a host or a network and another network, such as the Internet, and can be implemented as software running on the machine, hooking into the network stack (or, in the case of most UNIX-based operating systems such as Linux, built into the operating system kernel) to provide real time filtering and blocking. Another implementation is a so-called "physical firewall", which consists of a separate machine filtering network traffic. Firewalls are common amongst machines that are permanently connected to the Internet.

Some organizations are turning to big data platforms, such as Apache Hadoop, to extend data accessibility and machine learning to detect advanced persistent threats.[88][89]

However, relatively few organisations maintain computer systems with effective detection systems, and fewer still have organised response mechanisms in place. As result, as Reuters points out: "Companies for the first time report they are losing more through electronic theft of data than physical stealing of assets". [90] The primary obstacle to effective eradication of cyber crime could be traced to excessive reliance on firewalls and other automated "detection" systems. Yet it is basic evidence gathering by using packet capture appliances that puts criminals behind bars.[*citation needed*]

Computer Security, Computer Protection (countermeasures), Vulnerability Management

Vulnerability management is the cycle of identifying, and remediating or mitigating vulnerabilities",[91] especially in software and firmware. Vulnerability management is integral to computer security and network security.

Vulnerabilities can be discovered with a vulnerability scanner, which analyzes a computer system in search of known vulnerabilities,[92] such as open ports, insecure software configuration, and susceptibility to malware

Beyond vulnerability scanning, many organisations contract outside security auditors to run regular penetration tests against their systems to identify vulnerabilities. In some sectors this is a contractual requirement.[93]

Computer Security, Computer Protection (countermeasures), Vulnerability Management, Reducing Vulnerabilities

While formal verification of the correctness of computer systems is possible,[94][95] it is not yet common. Operating systems formally verified include seL4,[96] and SYSGO's PikeOS[97][98] – but these make up a very small percentage of the market.

Cryptography properly implemented is now virtually impossible to directly break. Breaking them requires some non-cryptographic input, such as a stolen key, stolen plaintext (at either end of the transmission), or some other extra cryptanalytic information.

Two factor authentication is a method for mitigating unauthorized access to a system or sensitive information. It requires "something you know"; a password or PIN, and "something you have"; a card, dongle, cellphone, or other piece of hardware. This increases security as an unauthorized person needs both of these to gain access.

Social engineering and direct computer access (physical) attacks can only be prevented by non-computer means, which can be difficult to enforce, relative to the sensitivity of the information. Training is often involved to help mitigate this risk, but even in a highly disciplined environments (e.g. military organizations), social engineering attacks can still be difficult to foresee and prevent.

Enoculation, derived from Inoculation theory, seeks to prevent social engineering and other fraudulent tricks or traps by instilling a resistance to persuasion attempts through exposure to similar or related attempts.[99]

It is possible to reduce an attacker's chances by keeping systems up to date with security patches and updates, using a security scanner or/and hiring competent people responsible for security. The effects of data loss/damage can be reduced by careful backing up and insurance.

Computer Security, Computer Protection (countermeasures), Vulnerability Management, Hardware Protection Mechanisms

While hardware may be a source of insecurity, such as with microchip vulnerabilities maliciously introduced during the manufacturing process,[100][101] hardware-based or assisted computer security also offers an alternative to software-only computer security. Using devices and methods such as dongles, trusted platform modules, intrusion-aware cases, drive locks, disabling USB ports, and mobile-enabled access may be considered more secure due to the physical access (or sophisticated backdoor access) required in order to be compromised. Each of these is covered in more detail below.

- USB dongles are typically used in software licensing schemes to unlock software capabilities,[102] but they can also be seen as a way to prevent unauthorized access to a computer or other device's software. The dongle, or key, essentially creates a secure encrypted tunnel between the software application and the key. The principle is that an encryption scheme on the dongle, such as Advanced Encryption Standard (AES) provides a stronger measure of security, since it is harder to hack and replicate the dongle than to simply copy the native software to another machine and use it. Another security application for dongles is to use them for accessing web-based content such as cloud software or Virtual Private Networks (VPNs).[103] In addition, a USB dongle can be configured to lock or unlock a computer.[104]
- Trusted platform modules (TPMs) secure devices by integrating cryptographic capabilities onto access devices, through the use of microprocessors, or so-called computers-on-a-chip. TPMs used in conjunction with server-side software offer a way to detect and authenticate hardware devices, preventing unauthorized network and data access.[105]
- Computer case intrusion detection refers to a push-button switch which is triggered when a computer case is opened. The firmware or BIOS is programmed to show an alert to the operator when the computer is booted up the next time.

- Drive locks are essentially software tools to encrypt hard drives, making them inaccessible to thieves.[106] Tools exist specifically for encrypting external drives as well.[107]
- Disabling USB ports is a security option for preventing unauthorized and malicious access to an otherwise secure computer. Infected USB dongles connected to a network from a computer inside the firewall are considered by the magazine Network World as the most common hardware threat facing computer networks.[108]
- Mobile-enabled access devices are growing in popularity due to the ubiquitous nature of cell phones. Built-in capabilities such as Bluetooth, the newer Bluetooth low energy (LE), Near field communication (NFC) on non-iOS devices and biometric validation such as thumb print readers, as well as QR code reader software designed for mobile devices, offer new, secure ways for mobile phones to connect to access control systems. These control systems provide computer security and can also be used for controlling access to secure buildings.[109]

Computer Security, Computer Protection (countermeasures), Vulnerability Management, Secure Operating Systems

One use of the term "computer security" refers to technology that is used to implement secure operating systems. In the 1980s the United States Department of Defense (DoD) used the "Orange Book"[110] standards, but the current international standard ISO/IEC 15408, "Common Criteria" defines a number of progressively more stringent Evaluation Assurance Levels. Many common operating systems meet the EAL4 standard of being "Methodically Designed, Tested and Reviewed", but the formal verification required for the highest levels means that they are uncommon. An example of an EAL6 ("Semiformally Verified Design and Tested") system is Integrity-178B, which is used in the Airbus A380[111] and several military jets.[112]

Computer Security, Computer Protection (countermeasures), Vulnerability Management, Secure Coding

In software engineering, secure coding aims to guard against the accidental introduction of security vulnerabilities. It is also possible to create software designed from the ground up to be secure. Such systems are "secure by design". Beyond this, formal verification aims to prove the correctness of the algorithms underlying a system;[113] important for cryptographic protocols for example.

Computer Security, Computer Protection (countermeasures), Vulnerability Management, Capabilities and Access Control Lists

Within computer systems, two of many security models capable of enforcing privilege separation are access control lists (ACLs) and capability-based security. Using ACLs to confine programs has been proven to be insecure in many situations, such as if the host computer can be tricked into indirectly allowing restricted file access, an issue known as the confused deputy problem. It has also been shown that the promise of ACLs of giving access to an object to only one person can never be guaranteed in practice. Both of these problems are resolved by capabilities. This does not mean practical flaws exist in all ACL-based systems, but only that the designers of certain utilities must take responsibility to ensure that they do not introduce flaws.[*citation needed*]

Capabilities have been mostly restricted to research operating systems, while commercial OSs still use ACLs. Capabilities can, however, also be implemented at the language level, leading to a style of programming that is essentially a refinement of standard object-oriented design. An open source project in the area is the E language.

The most secure computers are those not connected to the Internet and shielded from any interference. In the real world, the most secure systems are operating systems where security is not an add-on.

Computer Security, Computer Protection (countermeasures), Vulnerability Management, Response to Breaches

Responding forcefully to attempted security breaches (in the manner that one would for attempted physical security breaches) is often very difficult for a variety of reasons:

- Identifying attackers is difficult, as they are often in a different jurisdiction to the systems they attempt to breach, and operate through proxies, temporary anonymous dial-up accounts, wireless connections, and other anonymising procedures which make backtracing difficult and are often located in yet another jurisdiction. If they successfully breach security, they are often able to delete logs to cover their tracks.
- The sheer number of attempted attacks is so large that organisations cannot spend time pursuing each attacker (a typical home user with a permanent (e.g., cable modem) connection will be attacked at least several times per day, so more attractive targets could be presumed to see many more). Note however, that most of the sheer bulk of these attacks are made by automated vulnerability scanners and computer worms.
- Law enforcement officers are often unfamiliar with information technology, and so lack the skills and interest in pursuing attackers. There are also budgetary constraints. It has been argued that the high cost of technology, such as DNA testing, and improved forensics mean less money for other kinds of law enforcement, so the overall rate of criminals not getting dealt with goes up as the cost of the technology increases. In addition, the identification of attackers across a network may require logs from various points in the network and in many countries, the release of these records to law enforcement (with the exception of being voluntarily surrendered by a network administrator or a system administrator) requires a search warrant and, depending on the circumstances, the legal proceedings required can be drawn out to the point where the records are either regularly destroyed, or the information is no longer relevant.

Computer Security, Terminology

The following terms used with regards to engineering secure systems are explained below.

- Access authorization restricts access to a computer to the group of users through the use of authentication systems. These systems can protect either the whole computer – such as through an interactive login screen – or individual services, such as an FTP server. There are many methods for identifying and authenticating users, such as passwords, identification cards, and, more recently, smart cards and biometric systems.
- Anti-virus software consists of computer programs that attempt to identify, thwart and eliminate

computer viruses and other malicious software (malware).

- Applications are executable code, so general practice is to disallow users the power to install them; to install only those which are known to be reputable – and to reduce the attack surface by installing as few as possible. They are typically run with least privilege, with a robust process in place to identify, test and install any released security patches or updates for them.
- Authentication techniques can be used to ensure that communication end-points are who they say they are.]
- Automated theorem proving and other verification tools can enable critical algorithms and code used in secure systems to be mathematically proven to meet their specifications.
- Backups are one or more copies kept of important computer files. Typically multiple copies, (e.g. daily weekly and monthly), will be kept in different location away from the original, so that they are secure from damage if the original location has its security breached by an attacker, or is destroyed or damaged by natural disasters.
- Capability and access control list techniques can be used to ensure privilege separation and mandatory access control. This section discusses their use.
- Chain of trust techniques can be used to attempt to ensure that all software loaded has been certified as authentic by the system's designers.
- Confidentiality is the nondisclosure of information except to another authorized person.[196]
- Cryptographic techniques can be used to defend data in transit between systems, reducing the probability that data exchanged between systems can be intercepted or modified.
- Cyberwarfare is an internet-based conflict that involves politically motivated attacks on information and information systems. Such attacks can, for example, disable official websites and networks, disrupt or disable essential services, steal or alter classified data, and cripple financial systems.
- Data integrity is the accuracy and consistency of stored data, indicated by an absence of any alteration in data between two updates of a data record.[197]

- Cryptographic techniques involve transforming information, scrambling it so it becomes unreadable during transmission. The intended recipient can unscramble the message; ideally, eavesdroppers cannot.

- Encryption is used to protect the message from the eyes of others. Cryptographically secure ciphers are designed to make any practical attempt of breaking infeasible. Symmetric-key ciphers are suitable for bulk encryption using shared keys, and public-key encryption using digital certificates can provide a practical solution for the problem of securely communicating when no key is shared in advance.
- Endpoint security software helps networks to prevent exfiltration (data theft) and virus infection at network entry points made vulnerable by the prevalence of potentially infected portable computing devices, such as laptops and mobile devices, and external storage devices, such as USB drives.[198]
- Firewalls serve as a gatekeeper system between networks, allowing only traffic that matches defined rules. They often include detailed logging, and may include intrusion detection and intrusion prevention features. They are near-universal between company local area networks and the Internet, but can also be used internally to impose traffic rules between networks if network segmentation is configured.
- Honey pots are computers that are intentionally left vulnerable to attack by crackers. They can be used to catch crackers and to identify their techniques.
- Intrusion-detection systems can scan a network for people that are on the network but who should not be there or are doing things that they should not be doing, for example trying a lot of passwords

to gain access to the network.

- A microkernel is an approach to operating system design which has only the near-minimum amount of code running at the most privileged level – and runs other elements of the operating system such as device drivers, protocol stacks and file systems, in the safer, less privileged user space.
- Pinging. The standard "ping" application can be used to test if an IP address is in use. If it is, attackers may then try a port scan to detect which services are exposed.
- A port scan is used to probe an IP address for open ports, and hence identify network services running there.
- Social engineering is the use of the use of deception to manipulate individuals to breach security.

Mobile Security

Mobile security, or also mobile device security has become increasingly important in mobile computing. Of particular concern is the security of personal and business information now stored on smartphones.

More and more users and businesses use smartphones to communicate, but also to plan and organize their users' work and also private life. Within companies, these technologies are causing profound changes in the organization of information systems and therefore they have become the source of new risks. Indeed, smartphones collect and compile an increasing amount of sensitive information to which access must be controlled to protect the privacy of the user and the intellectual property of the company.

All smartphones, as computers, are preferred targets of attacks. These attacks exploit weaknesses inherent in smartphones that can come from the communication mode—like Short Message Service (SMS, aka text messaging), Multimedia Messaging Service (MMS), wifi, Bluetooth and GSM, the *de facto* global standard for mobile communications. There are also exploits that target software vulnerabilities in the browser or operating system. And some malicious software relies on the weak knowledge of an average user. According to a finding by McAfee in 2008, 11.6% users had heard of someone else being affected by mobile malware, but only 2.1% had personal experience on such problem.[1] However, this number is expected to grow.

Security countermeasures are being developed and applied to smartphones, from security in different layers of software to the dissemination of information to end users. There are good practices to be observed at all levels, from design to use, through the development of operating systems, software layers, and downloadable apps.

Mobile Security, Challenges of Mobile Security, Threats

A smartphone user is exposed to various threats when they use their phone. In just the last two-quarters of 2012, the number of unique mobile threats grew by 261%, according to ABI Research.[2] These threats can disrupt the operation of the smartphone, and transmit or modify user data. So applications must guarantee privacy and integrity of the information they handle. In addition, since some apps could themselves be malware, their functionality and activities should be limited (for example, restricting the apps from accessing location information via GPS, blocking access to the user's address book, preventing the transmission of data on the network, sending SMS messages that are billed to the user, etc.).

There are three prime targets for attackers:[3]

- Data: smartphones are devices for data management, and may contain sensitive data like credit card numbers, authentication information, private information, activity logs (calendar, call logs);
- Identity: smartphones are highly customizable, so the device or its contents can easily be associated with a specific person. For example, every mobile device can transmit information related to the owner of the mobile phone contract,[*citation needed*] and an attacker may want to steal the identity of the owner of a smartphone to commit other offenses;
- Availability: attacking a smartphone can limit access to it and deprive the owner of its use.

The source of these attacks are the same actors found in the non-mobile computing space:[3]

- Professionals, whether commercial or military, who focus on the three targets mentioned above. They steal sensitive data from the general public, as well as undertake industrial espionage. They will also use the identity of those attacked to achieve other attacks;
- Thieves who want to gain income through data or identities they have stolen. The thieves will attack many people to increase their potential income;
- Black hat hackers who specifically attack availability.[4] Their goal is to develop viruses, and cause damage to the device.[5] In some cases, hackers have an interest in stealing data on devices.
- Grey hat hackers who reveal vulnerabilities.[6] Their goal is to expose vulnerabilities of the device. [7] Grey hat hackers do not intend on damaging the device or stealing data.[8]

Mobile Security, Challenges of Mobile Security, Consequences

When a smartphone is infected by an attacker, the attacker can attempt several things:

- The attacker can manipulate the smartphone as a zombie machine, that is to say, a machine with which the attacker can communicate and send commands which will be used to send unsolicited messages (spam) via sms or email;[9]
- The attacker can easily force the smartphone to make phone calls. For example, one can use the API (library that contains the basic functions not present in the smartphone) PhoneMakeCall by Microsoft, which collects telephone numbers from any source such as yellow pages, and then call them.[9] But the attacker can also use this method to call paid services, resulting in a charge to the owner of the smartphone. It is also very dangerous because the smartphone could call emergency services and thus disrupt those services;[9]
- A compromised smartphone can record conversations between the user and others and send them to a third party.[9] This can cause user privacy and industrial security problems;
- An attacker can also steal a user's identity, usurp their identity (with a copy of the user's sim card or even the telephone itself), and thus impersonate the owner. This raises security concerns in countries where smartphones can be used to place orders, view bank accounts or are used as an identity card; [9]
- The attacker can reduce the utility of the smartphone, by discharging the battery.[10] For example, they can launch an application that will run continuously on the smartphone processor, requiring a lot of energy and draining the battery. One factor that distinguishes mobile computing from traditional desktop PCs is their limited performance. Frank Stajano and Ross Anderson first

described this form of attack, calling it an attack of "battery exhaustion" or "sleep deprivation torture";[11]

- The attacker can prevent the operation and/or be starting of the smartphone by making it unusable. [12] This attack can either delete the boot scripts, resulting in a phone without a functioning OS, or modify certain files to make it unusable (e.g. a script that launches at startup that forces the smartphone to restart) or even embed a startup application that would empty the battery;[11]
- The attacker can remove the personal (photos, music, videos, etc.) or professional data (contacts, calendars, notes) of the user.[12]

Mobile Security, Attacks Based on Wi-Fi

An attacker can try to eavesdrop on Wi-Fi communications to derive information (e.g. username, password). This type of attack is not unique to smartphones, but they are very vulnerable to these attacks because very often the Wi-Fi is the only means of communication they have to access the internet. The security of wireless networks (WLAN) is thus an important subject. Initially, wireless networks were secured by WEP keys. The weakness of WEP is a short encryption key which is the same for all connected clients. In addition, several reductions in the search space of the keys have been found by researchers. Now, most wireless networks are protected by the WPA security protocol. WPA is based on the "Temporal Key Integrity Protocol (TKIP)" which was designed to allow migration from WEP to WPA on the equipment already deployed. The major improvements in security are the dynamic encryption keys. For small networks, the WPA is a "pre-shared key" which is based on a shared key. Encryption can be vulnerable if the length of the shared key is short. With limited opportunities for input (i.e. only the numeric keypad), mobile phone users might define short encryption keys that contain only numbers. This increases the likelihood that an attacker succeeds with a brute-force attack. The successor to WPA, called WPA2, is supposed to be safe enough to withstand a brute force attack.

As with GSM, if the attacker succeeds in breaking the identification key, it will be possible to attack not only the phone but also the entire network it is connected to.

Many smartphones for wireless LANs remember they are already connected, and this mechanism prevents the user from having to re-identify with each connection. However, an attacker could create a WIFI access point twin with the same parameters and characteristics as the real network. Using the fact that some smartphones remember the networks, they could confuse the two networks and connect to the network of the attacker who can intercept data if it does not transmit its data in encrypted form.[18][19][20]

Lasco is a worm that initially infects a remote device using the SIS file format.[21] SIS file format (Software Installation Script) is a script file that can be executed by the system without user interaction. The smartphone thus believes the file to come from a trusted source and downloads it, infecting the machine.[21]

Mobile Security, Attacks Based on Hardware Vulnerabilities, Electromagnetic Waveforms

In 2015, researchers at the French government agency Agence nationale de la sécurité des systèmes d'information (ANSSI) demonstrated the capability to trigger the voice interface of certain smartphones remotely by using "specific electromagnetic waveforms".[26] The exploit took advantage of antenna-properties of headphone wires while plugged into the audio-output jacks of the vulnerable smartphones and effectively spoofed audio input to inject commands via the audio interface.[26]

Mobile Security, Attacks Based on Hardware Vulnerabilities, Juice Jacking

Juice Jacking is a physical or hardware vulnerability specific to mobile platforms. Utilizing the dual purpose of the USB charge port, many devices have been susceptible to having data exfiltrated from, or malware installed onto a mobile device by utilizing malicious charging kiosks set up in public places or hidden in normal charge adapters.

Mobile Security, Password Cracking

In 2010, researcher from the University of Pennsylvania investigated the possibility of cracking a device's password through a smudge attack (literally imaging the finger smudges on the screen to discern the user's password).[27] The researchers were able to discern the device password up to 68% of the time under certain conditions.[27] Outsiders may perform over-the-shoulder on victims, such as watching specific keystrokes or pattern gestures, to unlock device password or passcode.

Mobile Security, Malicious Software (malware)

As smartphones are a permanent point of access to the internet (mostly on), they can be compromised as easily as computers with malware. A malware is a computer program that aims to harm the system in which it resides. Trojans, worms and viruses are all considered malware. A Trojan is a program that is on the smartphone and allows external users to connect discreetly. A worm is a program that reproduces on multiple computers across a network. A virus is malicious software designed to spread to other computers by inserting itself into legitimate programs and running programs in parallel. However, it must be said that the malware are far less numerous and important to smartphones as they are to computers.[28]

Nonetheless, recent studies show that the evolution of malware in smartphones have rocketed in the last few years posing a threat to analysis and detection.[29]

Mobile Security, the Three Phases of Malware Attacks

Typically an attack on a smartphone made by malware takes place in 3 phases: the infection of a host, the accomplishment of its goal, and the spread of the malware to other systems. Malware often uses the resources offered by the infected smartphones. It will use the output devices such as Bluetooth or infrared, but it may also use the address book or email address of the person to infect the user's acquaintances. The malware exploits the trust that is given to data sent by an acquaintance.

Mobile Security, the Three Phases of Malware Attacks, Infection

Infection is the means used by the malware to get into the smartphone, it can either use one of the faults previously presented or may use the gullibility of the user. Infections are classified into four classes according to their degree of user interaction:[30]

Explicit permission
> the most benign interaction is to ask the user if it is allowed to infect the machine, clearly indicating its potential malicious behavior. This is typical behavior of a proof of concept malware.

Implied permission
> this infection is based on the fact that the user has a habit of installing software. Most trojans try to seduce the user into installing attractive applications (games, useful applications etc.) that actually contain malware.

Common interaction
> this infection is related to a common behavior, such as opening an MMS or email.

No interaction
> the last class of infection is the most dangerous. Indeed, a worm that could infect a smartphone and could infect other smartphones without any interaction would be catastrophic.

Mobile Security, the Three Phases of Malware Attacks, Accomplishment of its Goal

Once the malware has infected a phone it will also seek to accomplish its goal, which is usually one of the following: monetary damage, damage data and/or device, and concealed damage:[31]

Monetary damages
> the attacker can steal user data and either sell them to the same user or sell to a third party.

Damage
> malware can partially damage the device, or delete or modify data on the device.

Concealed damage
> the two aforementioned types of damage are detectable, but the malware can also leave a backdoor for future attacks or even conduct wiretaps.

Mobile Security, the Three Phases of Malware Attacks, Spread to other Systems

Once the malware has infected a smartphone, it always aims to spread one way or another:[32]

- It can spread through proximate devices using Wi-Fi, Bluetooth and infrared;
- It can also spread using remote networks such as telephone calls or SMS or emails.

Mobile Security, Examples of Malware

Here are various malware that exist in the world of smartphones with a short description of each.

Mobile Security, Examples of Malware, Viruses and Trojans

- Cabir (also known as Caribe, SybmOS/Cabir, Symbian/Cabir and EPOC.cabir) is the name of a computer worm developed in 2004, designed to infect mobile phones running Symbian OS. It is believed to have been the first computer worm that can infect mobile phones

- Commwarrior, found March 7, 2005, was the first worm that can infect many machines from MMS. [12] It is sent as COMMWARRIOR.ZIP containing the file COMMWARRIOR.SIS. When this file is executed, Commwarrior attempts to connect to nearby devices by Bluetooth or infrared under a random name. It then attempts to send MMS message to the contacts in the smartphone with different header messages for each person, who receive the MMS and often open them without further verification.

- Phage is the first Palm OS virus discovered.[12] It transfers to the Palm from a PC via synchronization. It infects all applications in the smartphone and embeds its own code to function without the user and the system detecting it. All that the system will detect is that its usual applications are functioning.

- RedBrowser is a Trojan based on java.[12] The Trojan masquerades as a program called "RedBrowser" which allows the user to visit WAP sites without a WAP connection. During application installation, the user sees a request on their phone that the application needs permission to send messages. If the user accepts, RedBrowser can send SMS to paid call centers. This program uses the smartphone's connection to social networks (Facebook, Twitter, etc.) to get the contact information for the user's acquaintances (provided the required permissions have been given) and will send them messages.

- WinCE.PmCryptic.A is malicious software on Windows Mobile which aims to earn money for its authors. It uses the infestation of memory cards that are inserted in the smartphone to spread more effectively.[33]

- CardTrap is a virus that is available on different types of smartphone, which aims to deactivate the system and third party applications. It works by replacing the files used to start the smartphone and applications to prevent them from executing.[34] There are different variants of this virus such as Cardtrap.A for SymbOS devices. It also infects the memory card with malware capable of infecting Windows.

- Ghost Push is malicious software on Android OS which automatically roots the android device and installs malicious applications directly to system partition then unroots the device to prevent users from removing the threat by master reset (The threat can be removed only by reflashing). It cripples the system resources, executes quickly, and is hard to detect.

Mobile Security, Examples of Malware, Ransomware

Mobile ransomware is a type of malware that locks users out of their mobile devices in a pay-to-unlock-your-device ploy, it has grown by leaps and bounds as a threat category since 2014.[35] Specific to mobile computing platforms, users are often less security-conscious, particularly as it pertains to scrutinizing applications and web links trusting the native protection capability of the mobile device operating system. Mobile ransomware poses a significant threat to businesses reliant on instant access and availability of their proprietary information and contacts. The likelihood of a traveling businessman paying a ransom to unlock their device is significantly higher since they are at a disadvantage given inconveniences such as timeliness and less likely direct access to IT staff.

Mobile Security, Examples of Malware, Spyware

- Flexispy is an application that can be considered as a trojan, based on Symbian. The program sends all information received and sent from the smartphone to a Flexispy server. It was originally created to protect children and spy on adulterous spouses.[12]

Mobile Security, Portability of Malware Across Platforms

There is a multitude of malware. This is partly due to the variety of operating systems on smartphones. However attackers can also choose to make their malware target multiple platforms, and malware can be found which attacks an OS but is able to spread to different systems.

To begin with, malware can use runtime environments like Java virtual machine or the .NET Framework. They can also use other libraries present in many operating systems.[36] Other malware carry several executable files in order to run in multiple environments and they utilize these during the propagation process. In practice, this type of malware requires a connection between the two operating systems to use as an attack vector. Memory cards can be used for this purpose, or synchronization software can be used to propagate the virus.

Mobile Security, Countermeasures

The security mechanisms in place to counter the threats described above are presented in this section. They are divided into different categories, as all do not act at the same level, and they range from the management of security by the operating system to the behavioral education of the user. The threats prevented by the various measures are not the same depending on the case. Considering the two cases mentioned above, in the first case one would protect the system from corruption by an application, and in the second case the installation of a suspicious software would be prevented.

Mobile Security, Countermeasures, Security in Operating Systems

The first layer of security in a smartphone is the operating system (OS). Beyond needing to handle the usual roles of an operating system (e.g. resource management, scheduling processes) on the device, it must also establish the protocols for introducing external applications and data without introducing risk.[*citation needed*]

A central paradigm in mobile operating systems is the idea of a sandbox. Since smartphones are currently designed to accommodate many applications, they must have mechanisms to ensure these applications are safe for the phone itself, for other applications and data on the system, and for the user. If a malicious program reaches a mobile device, the vulnerable area presented by the system must be as small as possible. Sandboxing extends this idea to compartmentalize different processes, preventing them from interacting and damaging each other. Based on the history of operating systems, sandboxing has different implementations. For example, where iOS will focus on limiting access to its public API for applications from the App Store by default, Managed Open In allows you to restrict which apps can access which types of data. Android bases its sandboxing on its legacy of Linux and TrustedBSD.

The following points highlight mechanisms implemented in operating systems, especially Android.

Rootkit Detectors

The intrusion of a rootkit in the system is a great danger in the same way as on a computer. It is important to prevent such intrusions, and to be able to detect them as often as possible. Indeed, there is concern that with this type of malicious program, the result could be a partial or complete bypass of the device security, and the acquisition of administrator rights by the attacker. If this happens, then nothing prevents the attacker from studying or disabling the safety features that were circumvented, deploying the applications they want, or disseminating a method of intrusion by a rootkit to a wider audience.[37][38] We can cite, as a defense mechanism, the Chain of trust in iOS. This mechanism relies on the signature of the different applications required to start the operating system, and a certificate signed by Apple. In the event that the signature checks are inconclusive, the device detects this and stops the boot-up.[39] If the Operating System is compromised due to Jailbreaking, root kit detection may not work if it is disabled by the Jailbreak method or software is loaded after Jailbreak disables Rootkit Detection.

Process isolation

Android uses mechanisms of user process isolation inherited from Linux. Each application has a user associated with it, and a tuple (UID, GID). This approach serves as a sandbox: while applications can be malicious, they can not get out of the sandbox reserved for them by their identifiers, and thus cannot interfere with the proper functioning of the system. For example, since it is impossible for a process to end the process of another user, an application can thus not stop the execution of another. [37][40][41][42][43]

File permissions

From the legacy of Linux, there are also filesystem permissions mechanisms. They help with sandboxing: a process can not edit any files it wants. It is therefore not possible to freely corrupt files necessary for the operation of another application or system. Furthermore, in Android there is the method of locking memory permissions. It is not possible to change the permissions of files installed on the SD card from the phone, and consequently it is impossible to install applications.[44][45][46]

Memory protection

In the same way as on a computer, memory protection prevents privilege escalation. Indeed, if a process managed to reach the area allocated to other processes, it could write in the memory of a process with rights superior to their own, with root in the worst case, and perform actions which are beyond its permissions on the system. It would suffice to insert function calls are authorized by the privileges of the malicious application.[43]

Development through runtime environments

Software is often developed in high-level languages, which can control what is being done by a running program. For example, Java Virtual Machines continuously monitor the actions of the execution threads they manage, monitor and assign resources, and prevent malicious actions. Buffer overflows can be prevented by these controls.[47][48][43]

Mobile Security, Countermeasures, Security Software

Above the operating system security, there is a layer of security software. This layer is composed of individual components to strengthen various vulnerabilities: prevent malware, intrusions, the identification of a user as a human, and user authentication. It contains software components that have learned from their experience with computer security; however, on smartphones, this software must deal with greater constraints (see limitations).

Antivirus and firewall

An antivirus software can be deployed on a device to verify that it is not infected by a known threat, usually by signature detection software that detects malicious executable files. A firewall, meanwhile, can watch over the existing traffic on the network and ensure that a malicious application does not seek to communicate through it. It may equally verify that an installed application does not seek to establish suspicious communication, which may prevent an intrusion attempt.[49][50][51][38]

Visual notifications

In order to make the user aware of any abnormal actions, such as a call they did not initiate, one can link some functions to a visual notification that is impossible to circumvent. For example, when a call is triggered, the called number should always be displayed. Thus, if a call is triggered by a malicious application, the user can see, and take appropriate action.

Turing test

In the same vein as above, it is important to confirm certain actions by a user decision. The Turing test is used to distinguish between a human and a virtual user, and it often comes as a captcha.

Biometric identification

Another method to use is biometrics.[52] Biometrics is a technique of identifying a person by means of their morphology(by recognition of the eye or face, for example) or their behavior (their signature or way of writing for example). One advantage of using biometric security is that users can avoid having to remember a password or other secret combination to authenticate and prevent malicious users from accessing their device. In a system with strong biometric security, only the primary user can access the smartphone.

Mobile Security, Countermeasures, Resource Monitoring in the Smartphone

When an application passes the various security barriers, it can take the actions for which it was designed. When such actions are triggered, the activity of a malicious application can be sometimes detected if one monitors the various resources used on the phone. Depending on the goals of the malware, the consequences of infection are not always the same; all malicious applications are not intended to harm the devices on which they are deployed. The following sections describe different ways to detect suspicious activity.[53]

Battery

Some malware is aimed at exhausting the energy resources of the phone. Monitoring the energy consumption of the phone can be a way to detect certain malware applications.[37]

Memory usage

Memory usage is inherent in any application. However, if one finds that a substantial proportion of memory is used by an application, it may be flagged as suspicious.

Network traffic

On a smartphone, many applications are bound to connect via the network, as part of their normal operation. However, an application using a lot of bandwidth can be strongly suspected of attempting to communicate a lot of information, and disseminate data to many other devices. This observation only allows a suspicion, because some legitimate applications can be very resource-intensive in terms of network communications, the best example being streaming video.

Services

One can monitor the activity of various services of a smartphone. During certain moments, some services should not be active, and if one is detected, the application should be suspected. For example, the sending of an SMS when the user is filming video: this communication does not make sense and is suspicious; malware may attempt to send SMS while its activity is masked.[54]

The various points mentioned above are only indications and do not provide certainty about the legitimacy of the activity of an application. However, these criteria can help target suspicious applications, especially if several criteria are combined.

Mobile Security, Countermeasures, Network Surveillance

Network traffic exchanged by phones can be monitored. One can place safeguards in network routing points in order to detect abnormal behavior. As the mobile's use of network protocols is much more constrained than that of a computer, expected network data streams can be predicted (e.g. the protocol for sending an SMS), which permits detection of anomalies in mobile networks.[55]

Spam filters

As is the case with email exchanges, we can detect a spam campaign through means of mobile communications (SMS, MMS). It is therefore possible to detect and minimize this kind of attempt by filters deployed on network infrastructure that is relaying these messages.

Encryption of stored or transmitted information

Because it is always possible that data exchanged can be intercepted, communications, or even information storage, can rely on encryption to prevent a malicious entity from using any data obtained during communications. However, this poses the problem of key exchange for encryption algorithms, which requires a secure channel.

Telecom network monitoring

The networks for SMS and MMS exhibit predictable behavior, and there is not as much liberty compared with what one can do with protocols such as TCP or UDP. This implies that one cannot predict the use made of the common protocols of the web; one might generate very little traffic by consulting simple pages, rarely, or generate heavy traffic by using video streaming. On the other hand, messages exchanged via mobile phone have a framework and a specific model, and the user does not, in a normal case, have the freedom to intervene in the details of these communications. Therefore, if an abnormality is found in the flux of network data in the mobile networks, the potential threat can be quickly detected.

Mobile Security, Countermeasures, Manufacturer Surveillance

In the production and distribution chain for mobile devices, it is the responsibility of manufacturers to ensure that devices are delivered in a basic configuration without vulnerabilities. Most users are not experts and many of them are not aware of the existence of security vulnerabilities, so the device configuration as provided by manufacturers will be retained by many users. Below are listed several points which manufacturers should consider.

Remove debug mode
> Phones are sometimes set in a debug mode during manufacturing, but this mode must be disabled before the phone is sold. This mode allows access to different features, not intended for routine use by a user. Due to the speed of development and production, distractions occur and some devices are sold in debug mode. This kind of deployment exposes mobile devices to exploits that utilize this oversight.[56][57]

Default settings
> When a smartphone is sold, its default settings must be correct, and not leave security gaps. The default configuration is not always changed, so a good initial setup is essential for users. There are, for example, default configurations that are vulnerable to denial of service attacks.[37][58]

Security audit of apps
> Along with smart phones, appstores have emerged. A user finds themselves facing a huge range of applications. This is especially true for providers who manage appstores because they are tasked with examining the apps provided, from different points of view (e.g. security, content). The security audit should be particularly cautious, because if a fault is not detected, the application can spread very quickly within a few days, and infect a significant number of devices.[37]

Detect suspicious applications demanding rights
> When installing applications, it is good to warn the user against sets of permissions that, grouped together, seem potentially dangerous, or at least suspicious. Frameworks like such as Kirin, on Android, attempt to detect and prohibit certain sets of permissions.[59]

Revocation procedures
> Along with appstores appeared a new feature for mobile apps: remote revocation. First developed by Android, this procedure can remotely and globally uninstall an application, on any device that has it. This means the spread of a malicious application that managed to evade security checks can be immediately stopped when the threat is discovered.[60][61]

Avoid heavily customized systems
> Manufacturers are tempted to overlay custom layers on existing operating systems, with the dual purpose of offering customized options and disabling or charging for certain features. This has the dual effect of risking the introduction of new bugs in the system, coupled with an incentive for users to modify the systems to circumvent the manufacturer's restrictions. These systems are rarely as stable and reliable as the original, and may suffer from phishing attempts or other exploits.[*citation needed*]

Improve software patch processes

New versions of various software components of a smartphone, including operating systems, are regularly published. They correct many flaws over time. Nevertheless, manufacturers often do not deploy these updates to their devices in a timely fashion, and sometimes not at all. Thus, vulnerabilities persist when they could be corrected, and if they are not, since they are known, they are easily exploitable.[59]

Mobile Security, Countermeasures, User Awareness

Much malicious behavior is allowed by the carelessness of the user. From simply not leaving the device without a password, to precise control of permissions granted to applications added to the smartphone, the user has a large responsibility in the cycle of security: to not be the vector of intrusion. This precaution is especially important if the user is an employee of a company that stores business data on the device. Detailed below are some precautions that a user can take to manage security on a smartphone.

A recent survey by internet security experts BullGuard showed a lack of insight into the rising number of malicious threats affecting mobile phones, with 53% of users claiming that they are unaware of security software for Smartphones. A further 21% argued that such protection was unnecessary, and 42% admitted it hadn't crossed their mind ("Using APA," 2011). These statistics show consumers are not concerned about security risks because they believe it is not a serious problem. The key here is to always remember smartphones are effectively handheld computers and are just as vulnerable.

Being skeptical

A user should not believe everything that may be presented, as some information may be phishing or attempting to distribute a malicious application. It is therefore advisable to check the reputation of the application that they want to buy before actually installing it.[62]

Permissions given to applications

The mass distribution of applications is accompanied by the establishment of different permissions mechanisms for each operating system. It is necessary to clarify these permissions mechanisms to users, as they differ from one system to another, and are not always easy to understand. In addition, it is rarely possible to modify a set of permissions requested by an application if the number of permissions is too great. But this last point is a source of risk because a user can grant rights to an application, far beyond the rights it needs. For example, a note taking application does not require access to the geolocation service. The user must ensure the privileges required by an application during installation and should not accept the installation if requested rights are inconsistent.[63][58][64]

Be careful

Protection of a user's phone through simple gestures and precautions, such as locking the smartphone when it is not in use, not leaving their device unattended, not trusting applications, not storing sensitive data, or encrypting sensitive data that cannot be separated from the device.[65][66]

Ensure data

Smartphones have a significant memory and can carry several gigabytes of data. The user must be careful about what data it carries and whether they should be protected. While it is usually not dramatic if a song is copied, a file containing bank information or business data can be more risky. The user must have the prudence to avoid the transmission of sensitive data on a smartphone, which can be easily stolen. Furthermore, when a user gets rid of a device, they must be sure to remove all personal data first.[67]

These precautions are measures that leave no easy solution to the intrusion of people or malicious applications in a smartphone. If users are careful, many attacks can be defeated, especially phishing and applications seeking only to obtain rights on a device.

Mobile Security, Countermeasures, Centralized Storage of Text Messages

One form of mobile protection allows companies to control the delivery and storage of text messages, by hosting the messages on a company server, rather than on the sender or receiver's phone. When certain conditions are met, such as an expiration date, the messages are deleted.[68]

Mobile Security, Countermeasures, Limitations of Certain Security Measures

The security mechanisms mentioned in this article are to a large extent inherited from knowledge and experience with computer security. The elements composing the two device types are similar, and there are common measures that can be used, such as antivirus software and firewalls. However, the implementation of these solutions is not necessarily possible or at least highly constrained within a mobile device. The reason for this difference is the technical resources offered by computers and mobile devices: even though the computing power of smartphones is becoming faster, they have other limitations than their computing power.

- Single-task system: Some operating systems, including some still commonly used, are single-tasking. Only the foreground task is executed. It is difficult to introduce applications such as antivirus and firewall on such systems, because they could not perform their monitoring while the user is operating the device, when there would be most need of such monitoring.
- Energy autonomy: A critical one for the use of a smartphone is energy autonomy. It is important that the security mechanisms not consume battery resources, without which the autonomy of devices will be affected dramatically, undermining the effective use of the smartphone.
- Network directly related to battery life, network utilization should not be too high. It is indeed one of the most expensive resources, from the point of view of energy consumption. Nonetheless, some calculations may need to be relocated to remote servers in order to preserve the battery. This balance can make implementation of certain intensive computation mechanisms a delicate proposition.[69]

Furthermore, it should be noted that it is common to find that updates exist, or can be developed or deployed, but this is not always done. One can, for example, find a user who does not know that there is a newer version of the operating system compatible with the smartphone, or a user may discover known vulnerabilities that are not corrected until the end of a long development cycle, which allows time to exploit the loopholes.[57]

Mobile Security, Countermeasures, Next Generation of Mobile Security

There is expected to be four mobile environments that will make up the security framework:

Rich operating system

In this category will fall traditional Mobile OS like Android, iOS, Symbian OS or Windows Phone. They will provide the traditional functionaity and security of an OS to the applications.

Secure Operating System (Secure OS)

A secure kernel which will run in parallel with a fully featured Rich OS, on the same processor core. It will include drivers for the Rich OS ("normal world") to communicate with the secure kernel ("secure world"). The trusted infrastructure could include interfaces like the display or keypad to regions of PCI-E address space and memories.

Trusted Execution Environment (TEE)

Made up of hardware and software. It helps in the control of access rights and houses sensitive applications, which need to be isolated from the Rich OS. It effectively acts as a firewall between the "normal world" and "secure world".

Secure Element (SE)

The SE consists of tamper resistant hardware and associated software. It can provide high levels of security and work in tandem with the TEE. The SE will be mandatory for hosting proximity payment applications or official electronic signatures.

Security Applications (SA)

Numerous security applications are available on App Stores providing services of protection from viruses and performing vulnerability assessment.[70]

Computer Virus

A computer virus is a type of malicious software program ("malware") that, when executed, replicates itself by modifying other computer programs and inserting its own code.[1] Infected computer programs can include, as well, data files, or the "boot" sector of the hard drive. When this replication succeeds, the affected areas are then said to be "infected" with a computer virus.[2][3][4]

Virus writers use social engineering deceptions and exploit detailed knowledge of security vulnerabilities to initially infect systems and to spread the virus. The vast majority of viruses target systems running Microsoft Windows,[5][6][7] employing a variety of mechanisms to infect new hosts,[8] and often using complex anti-detection/stealth strategies to evade antivirus software.[9][10][11][12] Motives for creating viruses can include seeking profit (e.g., with ransomware), desire to send a political message, personal amusement, to demonstrate that a vulnerability exists in software, for sabotage and denial of service, or simply because they wish to explore cybersecurity issues, artificial life and evolutionary algorithms.[13]

Computer viruses currently cause billions of dollars' worth of economic damage each year,[14] due to causing system failure, wasting computer resources, corrupting data, increasing maintenance costs, etc. In response, free, open-source antivirus tools have been developed, and an industry of antivirus software has cropped up, selling or freely distributing virus protection to users of various operating systems.[15] As of 2005, even though no currently existing antivirus software was able to uncover all computer viruses (especially new ones), computer security researchers are actively searching for new ways to enable antivirus solutions to more effectively detect emerging viruses, before they have already become widely distributed.[16]

The term "virus" is also commonly, but erroneously, used to refer to other types of malware. "Malware" encompasses computer viruses along with many other forms of malicious software, such as computer "worms", ransomware, trojan horses, keyloggers, rootkits, spyware, adware, malicious Browser Helper Object (BHOs) and other malicious software. The majority of active malware threats are actually trojan horse programs or computer worms rather than computer viruses. The term computer virus, coined by Fred Cohen in 1985, is a misnomer.[17] Viruses often perform some type of harmful activity on infected host computers, such as acquisition of hard disk space or central processing unit (CPU) time, accessing private information (e.g., credit card numbers), corrupting data, displaying political or humorous messages on the user's screen, spamming their e-mail contacts, logging their keystrokes, or even rendering the computer useless. However, not all viruses carry a destructive "payload" and attempt to hide themselves—the defining characteristic of viruses is that they are self-replicating computer programs which modify other software without user consent.

Computer Virus, Historical Development, Early Academic Work on Self-replicating Programs

The first academic work on the theory of self-replicating computer programs[18] was done in 1949 by John von Neumann who gave lectures at the University of Illinois about the "Theory and Organization of Complicated Automata". The work of von Neumann was later published as the "Theory of self-reproducing automata". In his essay von Neumann described how a computer program could be designed to reproduce itself.[19] Von Neumann's design for a self-reproducing computer program is considered the world's first computer virus, and he is considered to be the theoretical "father" of computer virology.[20] In 1972, Veith Risak, directly building on von Neumann's work on self-replication, published his article "Selbstreproduzierende Automaten mit minimaler Informationsübertragung" (Self-reproducing automata with minimal information exchange).[21] The article describes a fully functional virus written in assembler programming language for a SIEMENS 4004/35 computer system. In 1980 Jürgen Kraus wrote his diplom thesis "Selbstreproduktion bei Programmen" (Self-reproduction of programs) at the University of Dortmund.[22] In his work Kraus postulated that computer programs can behave in a way similar to biological viruses.

Computer Virus, Historical Development, First Examples

The Creeper virus was first detected on ARPANET, the forerunner of the Internet, in the early 1970s.[23] Creeper was an experimental self-replicating program written by Bob Thomas at BBN Technologies in 1971.[24] Creeper used the ARPANET to infect DEC PDP-10 computers running the TENEX operating system.[25] Creeper gained access via the ARPANET and copied itself to the remote system where the message, "I'm the creeper, catch me if you can!" was displayed. The *Reaper* program was created to delete Creeper.[26] In fiction, the 1973 Michael Crichton sci-fi movie *Westworld* made an early mention of the concept of a computer virus, being a central plot theme that causes androids to run amok.[27] Alan Oppenheimer's character summarizes the problem by stating that "...there's a clear pattern here which suggests an analogy to an infectious disease process, spreading from one...area to the next." To which the replies are stated: "Perhaps there are superficial similarities to disease" and, "I must confess I find it difficult to believe in a disease of machinery."[28] (Crichton's earlier work, the 1969 novel *The Andromeda Strain* and 1971 film version of it were about a biological virus-like disease that threatened the human race.)

In 1982, a program called "Elk Cloner" was the first personal computer virus to appear "in the wild"—that is, outside the single computer or [computer] lab where it was created.[29] Written in 1981 by Richard Skrenta while in the ninth grade at Mount Lebanon High School near Pittsburgh, it attached itself to the Apple DOS 3.3 operating system and spread via floppy disk.[29][30] This virus, created as a practical joke when Skrenta was still in high school, was injected in a game on a floppy disk. On its 50th use the Elk Cloner virus would be activated, infecting the personal computer and displaying a short poem beginning "Elk Cloner: The program with a personality." In 1984 Fred Cohen from the University of Southern California wrote his paper "Computer Viruses – Theory and Experiments".[31] It was the first paper to explicitly call a self-reproducing program a "virus", a term introduced by Cohen's mentor Leonard Adleman. In 1987, Fred Cohen published a demonstration that there is no algorithm that can perfectly detect all possible viruses.[32] Fred Cohen's theoretical compression virus[33] was an example of a virus which was not malicious software (malware), but was putatively benevolent (well-intentioned). However, antivirus professionals do not accept the concept of "benevolent viruses", as any desired function can be implemented without involving a virus (automatic compression, for instance, is available under the Windows operating system at the choice of the user). Any virus will by definition make unauthorised changes to a computer, which is undesirable even if no damage is done or intended. On page one of *Dr Solomon's Virus Encyclopaedia*, the undesirability of viruses, even those that do nothing but reproduce, is thoroughly explained.[34]

An article that describes "useful virus functionalities" was published by J. B. Gunn under the title "Use of virus functions to provide a virtual APL interpreter under user control" in 1984.[35] The first IBM PC virus in the "wild" was a boot sector virus dubbed (c)Brain,[36] created in 1986 by the Farooq Alvi Brothers in Lahore, Pakistan, reportedly to deter unauthorized copying of the software they had written.[37] The first virus to specifically target Microsoft Windows, WinVir was discovered in April 1992, two years after the release of Windows 3.0.[38] The virus did not contain any Windows API calls, instead relying on DOS interrupts. A few years later, in February 1996, Australian hackers from the virus-writing crew VLAD created the Bizatch virus (also known as "Boza" virus), which was the first known virus to target Windows 95. In late 1997 the encrypted, memory-resident stealth virus Win32.Cabanas was released—the first known virus that targeted Windows NT (it was also able to infect Windows 3.0 and Windows 9x hosts).[39]

Even home computers were affected by viruses. The first one to appear on the Commodore Amiga was a boot sector virus called SCA virus, which was detected in November 1987.[40] The first social networking virus, Win32.5-0-1, was created by Matt Larose on August 15, 2001.[41] The virus specifically targeted users of MSN Messenger and online bulletin boards. Users would be required to click on a link to activate the virus, which would then send an email containing user data to an anonymous email address, which was later found to be owned by Larose. Data sent would contain items such as user IP address and email addresses, contacts, website browsing history, and commonly used phrases. In 2008, larger websites used part of the Win32.5-0-1 code to track web users advertising-related interests.

Computer Virus, Operations and Functions, Parts

A viable computer virus must contain a search routine, which locates new files or new disks which are worthwhile targets for infection. Secondly, every computer virus must contain a routine to copy itself into the program which the search routine locates.[42] The three main virus parts are:

Computer Virus, Operations and Functions, Parts, Infection Mechanism

Infection mechanism (also called 'infection vector'), is how the virus spreads or propagates. A virus typically has a search routine, which locates new files or new disks for infection.[43]

Computer Virus, Operations and Functions, Parts, Trigger

The trigger, which is also known as logic bomb, is the compiled version that could be activated any time an executable file with the virus is run that determines the event or condition for the malicious "payload" to be activated or delivered[44] such as a particular date, a particular time, particular presence of another program, capacity of the disk exceeding some limit,[45] or a double-click that opens a particular file.[46]

Computer Virus, Operations and Functions, Parts, Payload

The "payload" is the actual body or data that perform the actual malicious purpose of the virus. Payload activity might be noticeable (e.g., because it causes the system to slow down or "freeze"), as most of the time the "payload" itself is the harmful activity,[43] or some times non-destructive but distributive, which is called Virus hoax.[47]

Computer Virus, Operations and Functions, Phases

Virus phases is the life cycle of the computer virus, described by using an analogy to biology. This life cycle can be divided into four phases:

Computer Virus, Operations and Functions, Phases, Dormant Phase

The virus program is idle during this stage. The virus program has managed to access the target user's computer or software, but during this stage, the virus does not take any action. The virus will eventually be activated by the "trigger" which states which event will execute the virus, such as a date, the presence of another program or file, the capacity of the disk exceeding some limit or the user taking a certain action (e.g., double-clicking on a certain icon, opening an e-mail, etc.). Not all viruses have this stage.[43]

Computer Virus, Operations and Functions, Phases, Propagation Phase

The virus starts propagating, that is multiplying and replicating itself. The virus places a copy of itself into other programs or into certain system areas on the disk. The copy may not be identical to the propagating version; viruses often "morph" or change to evade detection by IT professionals and anti-virus software. Each infected program will now contain a clone of the virus, which will itself enter a propagation phase.[43]

Computer Virus, Operations and Functions, Phases, Triggering Phase

A dormant virus moves into this phase when it is activated, and will now perform the function for which it was intended. The triggering phase can be caused by a variety of system events, including a count of the number of times that this copy of the virus has made copies of itself.[43]

Computer Virus, Operations and Functions, Phases, Execution Phase

This is the actual work of the virus, where the "payload" will be released. It can be destructive such as deleting files on disk, crashing the system, or corrupting files or relatively harmless such as popping up humorous or political messages on screen.[43]

Computer Virus, Infection Targets and Replication Techniques

Computer viruses infect a variety of different subsystems on their host computers and software.[48] One manner of classifying viruses is to analyze whether they reside in binary executables (such as .EXE or .COM files), data files (such as Microsoft Word documents or PDF files), or in the boot sector of the host's hard drive (or some combination of all of these).[49][50]

Computer Virus, Infection Targets and Replication Techniques, Resident vs. Non-resident Viruses

A *memory-resident virus* (or simply "resident virus") installs itself as part of the operating system when executed, after which it remains in RAM from the time the computer is booted up to when it is shut down. Resident viruses overwrite interrupt handling code or other functions, and when the operating system attempts to access the target file or disk sector, the virus code intercepts the request and redirects the control flow to the replication module, infecting the target. In contrast, a *non-memory-resident virus* (or "non-resident virus"), when executed, scans the disk for targets, infects them, and then exits (i.e. it does not remain in memory after it is done executing).[51][52][53]

Computer Virus, Infection Targets and Replication Techniques, Macro Viruses

Many common applications, such as Microsoft Outlook and Microsoft Word, allow macro programs to be embedded in documents or emails, so that the programs may be run automatically when the document is opened. A *macro virus* (or "document virus") is a virus that is written in a macro language, and embedded into these documents so that when users open the file, the virus code is executed, and can infect the user's computer. This is one of the reasons that it is dangerous to open unexpected or suspicious attachments in e-mails.[54][55] While not opening attachments in e-mails from unknown persons or organizations can help to reduce the likelihood of contracting a virus, in some cases, the virus is designed so that the e-mail appears to be from a reputable organization (e.g., a major bank or credit card company).

Computer Virus, Infection Targets and Replication Techniques, Boot Sector Viruses

Boot sector viruses specifically target the boot sector and/or the Master Boot Record[56] (MBR) of the host's hard drive or removable storage media (flash drives, floppy disks, etc.).[49][57][58]

Computer Virus, Infection Targets and Replication Techniques, Email Virus

Email virus – A virus that specifically, rather than accidentally, uses the email system to spread. While virus infected files may be accidentally sent as email attachments, email viruses are aware of email system functions. They generally target a specific type of email system (Microsoft's Outlook is the most commonly used), harvest email addresses from various sources, and may append copies of themselves to all email sent, or may generate email messages containing copies of themselves as attachments.[59]

Computer Virus, Stealth Strategies

In order to avoid detection by users, some viruses employ different kinds of deception. Some old viruses, especially on the MS-DOS platform, make sure that the "last modified" date of a host file stays the same when the file is infected by the virus. This approach does not fool antivirus software, however, especially those which maintain and date cyclic redundancy checks on file changes.[60] Some viruses can infect files without increasing their sizes or damaging the files. They accomplish this by overwriting unused areas of executable files. These are called *cavity viruses*. For example, the CIH virus, or Chernobyl Virus, infects Portable Executable files. Because those files have many empty gaps, the virus, which was 1 KB in length, did not add to the size of the file.[61] Some viruses try to avoid detection by killing the tasks associated with antivirus software before it can detect them (for example, Conficker). In the 2010s, as computers and operating systems grow larger and more complex, old hiding techniques need to be updated or replaced. Defending a computer against viruses may demand that a file system migrate towards detailed and explicit permission for every kind of file access.[62]

Computer Virus, Stealth Strategies, Read Request Intercepts

While some antivirus software employ various techniques to counter stealth mechanisms, once the infection occurs any recourse to "clean" the system is unreliable. In Microsoft Windows operating systems, the NTFS file system is proprietary. This leaves antivirus software little alternative but to send a "read" request to Windows OS files that handle such requests. Some viruses trick antivirus software by intercepting its requests to the Operating system (OS). A virus can hide by intercepting the request to read the infected file, handling the request itself, and returning an uninfected version of the file to the antivirus software. The interception can occur by code injection of the actual operating system files that would handle the read request. Thus, an antivirus software attempting to detect the virus will either not be given permission to read the infected file, or, the "read" request will be served with the uninfected version of the same file.[63]

The only reliable method to avoid "stealth" viruses is to "boot" from a medium that is known to be "clean". Security software can then be used to check the dormant operating system files. Most security software relies on virus signatures, or they employ heuristics.[64][65] Security software may also use a database of file "hashes" for Windows OS files, so the security software can identify altered files, and request Windows installation media to replace them with authentic versions. In older versions of Windows, file cryptographic hash functions of Windows OS files stored in Windows—to allow file integrity/authenticity to be checked —could be overwritten so that the System File Checker would report that altered system files are authentic, so using file hashes to scan for altered files would not always guarantee finding an infection.[66]

Computer Virus, Stealth Strategies, Self-modification

Most modern antivirus programs try to find virus-patterns inside ordinary programs by scanning them for so-called *virus signatures*.[67] Unfortunately, the term is misleading, in that viruses do not possess unique signatures in the way that human beings do. Such a virus "signature" is merely a sequence of bytes that an antivirus program looks for because it is known to be part of the virus. A better term would be "search strings". Different antivirus programs will employ different search strings, and indeed different search methods, when identifying viruses. If a virus scanner finds such a pattern in a file, it will perform other checks to make sure that it has found the virus, and not merely a coincidental sequence in an innocent file, before it notifies the user that the file is infected. The user can then delete, or (in some cases) "clean" or "heal" the infected file. Some viruses employ techniques that make detection by means of signatures difficult but probably not impossible. These viruses modify their code on each infection. That is, each infected file contains a different variant of the virus.[*citation needed*]

Computer Virus, Stealth Strategies, Self-modification, Encrypted Viruses

One method of evading signature detection is to use simple encryption to encipher (encode) the body of the virus, leaving only the encryption module and a static cryptographic key in cleartext which does not change from one infection to the next.[68] In this case, the virus consists of a small decrypting module and an encrypted copy of the virus code. If the virus is encrypted with a different key for each infected file, the only part of the virus that remains constant is the decrypting module, which would (for example) be appended to the end. In this case, a virus scanner cannot directly detect the virus using signatures, but it can still detect the decrypting module, which still makes indirect detection of the virus possible. Since these would be symmetric keys, stored on the infected host, it is entirely possible to decrypt the final virus, but this is probably not required, since self-modifying code is such a rarity that it may be reason for virus scanners to at least "flag" the file as suspicious.[69] An old but compact way will be the use of arithmetic operation like addition or subtraction and the use of logical conditions such as XORing,[70] where each byte in a virus is with a constant, so that the exclusive-or operation had only to be repeated for decryption. It is suspicious for a code to modify itself, so the code to do the encryption/decryption may be part of the signature in many virus definitions.[69] A simpler older approach did not use a key, where the encryption consisted only of operations with no parameters, like incrementing and decrementing, bitwise rotation, arithmetic negation, and logical NOT.[70] Some viruses will employ a means of encryption inside an executable in which the virus is encrypted under certain events, such as the virus scanner being disabled for updates or the computer being rebooted. This is called cryptovirology. At said times, the executable will decrypt the virus and execute its hidden runtimes, infecting the computer and sometimes disabling the antivirus software.[*citation needed*]

Computer Virus, Stealth Strategies, Self-modification, Polymorphic Code

Polymorphic code was the first technique that posed a serious threat to virus scanners. Just like regular encrypted viruses, a polymorphic virus infects files with an encrypted copy of itself, which is decoded by a decryption module. In the case of polymorphic viruses, however, this decryption module is also modified on each infection. A well-written polymorphic virus therefore has no parts which remain identical between infections, making it very difficult to detect directly using "signatures".[71][72] Antivirus software can detect it by decrypting the viruses using an emulator, or by statistical pattern analysis of the encrypted virus body. To enable polymorphic code, the virus has to have a polymorphic engine (also called "mutating engine" or "mutation engine") somewhere in its encrypted body. See polymorphic code for technical detail on how such engines operate.[73]

Some viruses employ polymorphic code in a way that constrains the mutation rate of the virus significantly. For example, a virus can be programmed to mutate only slightly over time, or it can be programmed to refrain from mutating when it infects a file on a computer that already contains copies of the virus. The advantage of using such slow polymorphic code is that it makes it more difficult for antivirus professionals and investigators to obtain representative samples of the virus, because "bait" files that are infected in one run will typically contain identical or similar samples of the virus. This will make it more likely that the detection by the virus scanner will be unreliable, and that some instances of the virus may be able to avoid detection.

Computer Virus, Stealth Strategies, Self-modification, Metamorphic Code

To avoid being detected by emulation, some viruses rewrite themselves completely each time they are to infect new executables. Viruses that utilize this technique are said to be in metamorphic code. To enable metamorphism, a "metamorphic engine" is needed. A metamorphic virus is usually very large and complex. For example, W32/Simile consisted of over 14,000 lines of assembly language code, 90% of which is part of the metamorphic engine.[74][75]

Computer Virus, Vulnerabilities and Infection Vectors, Software Bugs

As software is often designed with security features to prevent unauthorized use of system resources, many viruses must exploit and manipulate security bugs, which are security defects in a system or application software, to spread themselves and infect other computers. Software development strategies that produce large numbers of "bugs" will generally also produce potential exploitable "holes" or "entrances" for the virus.

Computer Virus, Vulnerabilities and Infection Vectors, Social Engineering and Poor Security Practices

In order to replicate itself, a virus must be permitted to execute code and write to memory. For this reason, many viruses attach themselves to executable files that may be part of legitimate programs (see code injection). If a user attempts to launch an infected program, the virus' code may be executed simultaneously.[76] In operating systems that use file extensions to determine program associations (such as Microsoft Windows), the extensions may be hidden from the user by default. This makes it possible to create a file that is of a different type than it appears to the user. For example, an executable may be created and named "picture.png.exe", in which the user sees only "picture.png" and therefore assumes that this file is a digital image and most likely is safe, yet when opened, it runs the executable on the client machine.[77]

Computer Virus, Vulnerabilities and Infection Vectors, Vulnerability of Different Operating Systems

The vast majority of viruses target systems running Microsoft Windows. This is due to Microsoft's large market share of desktop computer users.[78] The diversity of software systems on a network limits the destructive potential of viruses and malware.[79] Open-source operating systems such as Linux allow users to choose from a variety of desktop environments, packaging tools, etc., which means that malicious code targeting any of these systems will only affect a subset of all users. Many Windows users are running the same set of applications, enabling viruses to rapidly spread among Microsoft Windows systems by targeting the same exploits on large numbers of hosts.[5][6][7][80]

While Linux and Unix in general have always natively prevented normal users from making changes to the operating system environment without permission, Windows users are generally not prevented from making these changes, meaning that viruses can easily gain control of the entire system on Windows hosts. This difference has continued partly due to the widespread use of administrator accounts in contemporary versions like Windows XP. In 1997, researchers created and released a virus for Linux—known as "Bliss". [81] Bliss, however, requires that the user run it explicitly, and it can only infect programs that the user has the access to modify. Unlike Windows users, most Unix users do not log in as an administrator, or "root user", except to install or configure software; as a result, even if a user ran the virus, it could not harm their operating system. The Bliss virus never became widespread, and remains chiefly a research curiosity. Its creator later posted the source code to Usenet, allowing researchers to see how it worked.[82]

Computer Virus, Countermeasures, Antivirus Software

Many users install antivirus software that can detect and eliminate known viruses when the computer attempts to download or run the executable file (which may be distributed as an email attachment, or on USB flash drives, for example). Some antivirus software blocks known malicious websites that attempt to install malware. Antivirus software does not change the underlying capability of hosts to transmit viruses. Users must update their software regularly to patch security vulnerabilities ("holes"). Antivirus software also needs to be regularly updated in order to recognize the latest threats. This is because malicious hackers and other individuals are always creating new viruses. The German AV-TEST Institute publishes evaluations of antivirus software for Windows[83] and Android.[84]

Examples of Microsoft Windows anti virus and anti-malware software include the optional Microsoft Security Essentials[85] (for Windows XP, Vista and Windows 7) for real-time protection, the Windows Malicious Software Removal Tool[86] (now included with Windows (Security) Updates on "Patch Tuesday", the second Tuesday of each month), and Windows Defender (an optional download in the case of Windows XP).[87] Additionally, several capable antivirus software programs are available for free download from the Internet (usually restricted to non-commercial use).[88] Some such free programs are almost as good as commercial competitors.[89] Common security vulnerabilities are assigned CVE IDs and listed in the US National Vulnerability Database. Secunia PSI[90] is an example of software, free for personal use, that will check a PC for vulnerable out-of-date software, and attempt to update it. Ransomware and phishing scam alerts appear as press releases on the Internet Crime Complaint Center noticeboard. Ransomware is a virus that posts a message on the user's screen saying that the screen or system will remain locked or unusable until a ransom payment is made. Phishing is a deception in which the malicious individual pretends to be a friend, computer security expert, or other benevolent individual, with the goal of convincing the targeted individual to reveal passwords or other personal information.

Other commonly used preventative measures include timely operating system updates, software updates, careful Internet browsing (avoiding shady websites), and installation of only trusted software.[91] Certain browsers flag sites that have been reported to Google and that have been confirmed as hosting malware by Google.[92][93]

There are two common methods that an antivirus software application uses to detect viruses, as described in the antivirus software article. The first, and by far the most common method of virus detection is using a list of virus signature definitions. This works by examining the content of the computer's memory (its Random Access Memory (RAM), and boot sectors) and the files stored on fixed or removable drives (hard drives, floppy drives, or USB flash drives), and comparing those files against a database of known virus "signatures". Virus signatures are just strings of code that are used to identify individual viruses; for each virus, the antivirus designer tries to choose a unique signature string that will not be found in a legitimate program. Different antivirus programs use different "signatures" to identify viruses. The disadvantage of this detection method is that users are only protected from viruses that are detected by signatures in their most recent virus definition update, and not protected from new viruses (see "zero-day attack").[94]

A second method to find viruses is to use a heuristic algorithm based on common virus behaviors. This method has the ability to detect new viruses for which antivirus security firms have yet to define a "signature", but it also gives rise to more false positives than using signatures. False positives can be disruptive, especially in a commercial environment, because it may lead to a company instructing staff not to use the company computer system until IT services has checked the system for viruses. This can slow down productivity for regular workers.

Computer Virus, Recovery Strategies and Methods

One may reduce the damage done by viruses by making regular backups of data (and the operating systems) on different media, that are either kept unconnected to the system (most of the time, as in a hard drive), read-only or not accessible for other reasons, such as using different file systems. This way, if data is lost through a virus, one can start again using the backup (which will hopefully be recent).[95] If a backup session on optical media like CD and DVD is closed, it becomes read-only and can no longer be affected by a virus (so long as a virus or infected file was not copied onto the CD/DVD). Likewise, an operating system on a bootable CD can be used to start the computer if the installed operating systems become unusable. Backups on removable media must be carefully inspected before restoration. The Gammima virus, for example, propagates via removable flash drives.[96][97]

Computer Virus, Recovery Strategies and Methods, Virus Removal

Many websites run by antivirus software companies provide free online virus scanning, with limited "cleaning" facilities (after all, the purpose of the websites is to sell antivirus products and services). Some websites—like Google subsidiary VirusTotal.com—allow users to upload one or more suspicious files to be scanned and checked by one or more antivirus programs in one operation.[98][99] Additionally, several capable antivirus software programs are available for free download from the Internet (usually restricted to non-commercial use).[100] Microsoft offers an optional free antivirus utility called Microsoft Security Essentials, a Windows Malicious Software Removal Tool that is updated as part of the regular Windows update regime, and an older optional anti-malware (malware removal) tool Windows Defender that has been upgraded to an antivirus product in Windows 8.

Some viruses disable System Restore and other important Windows tools such as Task Manager and CMD. An example of a virus that does this is CiaDoor. Many such viruses can be removed by rebooting the computer, entering Windows "safe mode" with networking, and then using system tools or Microsoft Safety Scanner.[101] System Restore on Windows Me, Windows XP, Windows Vista and Windows 7 can restore the registry and critical system files to a previous checkpoint. Often a virus will cause a system to "hang" or "freeze", and a subsequent hard reboot will render a system restore point from the same day corrupted. Restore points from previous days should work, provided the virus is not designed to corrupt the restore files and does not exist in previous restore points.[102][103]

Computer Virus, Recovery Strategies and Methods, Operating System Reinstallation

Microsoft's System File Checker (improved in Windows 7 and later) can be used to check for, and repair, corrupted system files.[104] Restoring an earlier "clean" (virus-free) copy of the entire partition from a cloned disk, a disk image, or a backup copy is one solution—restoring an earlier backup disk "image" is relatively simple to do, usually removes any malware, and may be faster than "disinfecting" the computer —or reinstalling and reconfiguring the operating system and programs from scratch, as described below, then restoring user preferences.[95] Reinstalling the operating system is another approach to virus removal. It may be possible to recover copies of essential user data by booting from a live CD, or connecting the hard drive to another computer and booting from the second computer's operating system, taking great care not to infect that computer by executing any infected programs on the original drive. The original hard drive can then be reformatted and the OS and all programs installed from original media. Once the system has been restored, precautions must be taken to avoid reinfection from any restored executable files.[105]

Computer Virus, Viruses and the Internet

Before computer networks became widespread, most viruses spread on removable media, particularly floppy disks. In the early days of the personal computer, many users regularly exchanged information and programs on floppies. Some viruses spread by infecting programs stored on these disks, while others installed themselves into the disk boot sector, ensuring that they would be run when the user booted the computer from the disk, usually inadvertently. Personal computers of the era would attempt to boot first from a floppy if one had been left in the drive. Until floppy disks fell out of use, this was the most successful infection strategy and boot sector viruses were the most common in the "wild" for many years. Traditional computer viruses emerged in the 1980s, driven by the spread of personal computers and the resultant increase in bulletin board system (BBS), modem use, and software sharing. Bulletin board–driven software sharing contributed directly to the spread of Trojan horse programs, and viruses were written to infect popularly traded software. Shareware and bootleg software were equally common vectors for viruses on BBSs.[106][107][108] Viruses can increase their chances of spreading to other computers by infecting files on a network file system or a file system that is accessed by other computers.[109]

Macro viruses have become common since the mid-1990s. Most of these viruses are written in the scripting languages for Microsoft programs such as Microsoft Word and Microsoft Excel and spread throughout Microsoft Office by infecting documents and spreadsheets. Since Word and Excel were also available for Mac OS, most could also spread to Macintosh computers. Although most of these viruses did not have the ability to send infected email messages, those viruses which did take advantage of the Microsoft Outlook Component Object Model (COM) interface.[110][111] Some old versions of Microsoft Word allow macros to replicate themselves with additional blank lines. If two macro viruses simultaneously infect a document, the combination of the two, if also self-replicating, can appear as a "mating" of the two and would likely be detected as a virus unique from the "parents".[112]

A virus may also send a web address link as an instant message to all the contacts (e.g., friends and colleagues' e-mail addresses) stored on an infected machine. If the recipient, thinking the link is from a friend (a trusted source) follows the link to the website, the virus hosted at the site may be able to infect this new computer and continue propagating.[113] Viruses that spread using cross-site scripting were first reported in 2002,[114] and were academically demonstrated in 2005.[115] There have been multiple instances of the cross-site scripting viruses in the "wild", exploiting websites such as MySpace (with the Samy worm) and Yahoo!.

Computer Worm

A computer worm is a standalone malware computer program that replicates itself in order to spread to other computers.[1] Often, it uses a computer network to spread itself, relying on security failures on the target computer to access it. Worms almost always cause at least some harm to the network, even if only by consuming bandwidth, whereas viruses almost always corrupt or modify files on a targeted computer.

Many worms that have been created are designed only to spread, and do not attempt to change the systems they pass through. However, as the Morris worm and Mydoom showed, even these "payload-free" worms can cause major disruption by increasing network traffic and other unintended effects.

Computer Worm, History

The actual term "worm" was first used in John Brunner's 1975 novel, *The Shockwave Rider*. In that novel, Nichlas Haflinger designs and sets off a data-gathering worm in an act of revenge against the powerful men who run a national electronic information web that induces mass conformity. "You have the biggest-ever worm loose in the net, and it automatically sabotages any attempt to monitor it... There's never been a worm with that tough a head or that long a tail!"[2]

On November 2, 1988, Robert Tappan Morris, a Cornell University computer science graduate student, unleashed what became known as the Morris worm, disrupting a large number of computers then on the Internet, guessed at the time to be one tenth of all those connected[3] During the Morris appeal process, the U.S. Court of Appeals estimated the cost of removing the virus from each installation was in the range of $200–53,000, and prompting the formation of the CERT Coordination Center[4] and Phage mailing list.[5] Morris himself became the first person tried and convicted under the 1986 Computer Fraud and Abuse Act. [6]

Computer Worm, Harm

Any code designed to do more than spread the worm is typically referred to as the "payload". Typical malicious payloads might delete files on a host system (e.g., the ExploreZip worm), encrypt files in a ransomware attack, or exfiltrate data such as confidential documents or passwords.

Probably the most common payload for worms is to install a backdoor. This allows the computer to be remotely controlled by the worm author as a "zombie". Networks of such machines are often referred to as botnets and are very commonly used for a range of malicious purposes, including sending spam or performing DoS attacks.[7][8][9][10][11]

Computer Worm, Countermeasures

Worms spread by exploiting vulnerabilities in operating systems. Vendors with security problems supply regular security updates[12], and if these are installed to a machine then the majority of worms are unable to spread to it. If a vulnerability is disclosed before the security patch released by the vendor, a zero-day attack is possible.

Users need to be wary of opening unexpected email,[13][14] and should not run attached files or programs, or visit web sites that are linked to such emails. However, as with the ILOVEYOU worm, and with the increased growth and efficiency of phishing attacks, it remains possible to trick the end-user into running malicious code.

Anti-virus and anti-spyware software are helpful, but must be kept up-to-date with new pattern files at least every few days. The use of a firewall is also recommended.

In the April–June 2008 issue of *IEEE Transactions on Dependable and Secure Computing*, computer scientists described a new and potentially effective way to combat internet worms. The researchers discovered how to contain worms that scanned the Internet randomly, looking for vulnerable hosts to infect. They found that the key was to use software to monitor the number of scans that machines on a network send out. When a machine started to send out too many scans, it was a sign that it has been infected, which allowed administrators to take it off line and check it for malware.[15][16] In addition, machine learning techniques can be used to detect new worms, by analyzing the behavior of the suspected computer.[17]

Users can minimize the threat posed by worms by keeping their computers' operating system and other software up to date, avoiding opening unrecognized or unexpected emails and running firewall and antivirus software.[18]

Mitigation techniques include:

- ACLs in routers and switches
- Packet-filters
- TCP Wrapper/ACL enabled network service daemons
- Nullroute

Computer Worm, Worms with Good Intent

Beginning with the very first research into worms at Xerox PARC, there have been attempts to create useful worms. Those worms allowed testing by John Shoch and Jon Hupp of the Ethernet principles on their network of Xerox Alto computers. The Nachi family of worms tried to download and install patches from Microsoft's website to fix vulnerabilities in the host system—by exploiting those same vulnerabilities.[19] In practice, although this may have made these systems more secure, it generated considerable network traffic, rebooted the machine in the course of patching it, and did its work without the consent of the computer's owner or user. Regardless of their payload or their writers' intentions, most security experts regard all worms as malware.

Several worms, like XSS worms, have been written to research how worms spread. For example, the effects of changes in social activity or user behavior. One study proposed what seems to be the first computer worm that operates on the second layer of the OSI model (Data link Layer), it utilizes topology information such as Content-addressable memory (CAM) tables and Spanning Tree information stored in switches to propagate and probe for vulnerable nodes until the enterprise network is covered.[20]

Trojan Horse

In computing, a Trojan horse, or Trojan, is any malicious computer program which misleads users of its true intent. The term is derived from the Ancient Greek story of the deceptive wooden horse that led to the fall of the city of Troy.[1][2][3][4][5]

Trojans are generally spread by some form of social engineering, for example where a user is duped into executing an e-mail attachment disguised to be unsuspicious, (e.g., a routine form to be filled in), or by drive-by download. Although their payload can be anything, many modern forms act as a backdoor, contacting a controller which can then have unauthorized access to the affected computer.[6] Trojans may allow an attacker to access users' personal information such as banking information, passwords, or personal identity (IP address). Ransomware attacks are often carried out using a Trojan.

Unlike computer viruses and worms, Trojans generally do not attempt to inject themselves into other files or otherwise propagate themselves.[7]

Trojan Horse, Operation of a Trojan

The principle of principle of least privilege should normally mean that most users do not have access to install a root kit, completely crash the computer or device, delete all data or format the disk - but many home users, and some corporate laptop users *will* have this power.

It can perform following task in user's computer or laptop

1. Block all the Anti Viruses

2. Block any program installation processes

3. Steal banking password or card information

4. Breach the security of all the devices

5. It infects all the other computers & devices connected to the same network, by using the infected computer as proxy this trojans send infection to other Computers and Devices.

6. It can send email password to hackers

7. Misuse of user's data like - email, photo, name and other apps like Facebook, skype etc.

8. It can infect multiple devices on the same network by infecting IP addresses.

9. Misuse the computer for crime activity and stealing other people's data

10. Block the inbuilt Firewall security

However, even if the user does not have any special access, they will still have access to read and write all document files which they have legitimate access to - and this is the only access ransomware needs to encrypt them. Similarly, they will may be easily able to read and exploit the user's banking information, and passwords to other systems.

It is also possible that some Trojans will be able to exploit a bug, design flaw or configuration oversight to achieve a privilege escalation to gain elevated access to resources.

If installed or run with elevated privileges a Trojan will generally have unlimited access. What it does with this power depends on the motives of the attacker.

Trojan Horse, Malicious Uses

Trojan in this way may require interaction with a malicious controller (not necessarily distributing the Trojan) to fulfill their purpose. It is possible for those involved with Trojans to scan computers on a network to locate any with a Trojan installed, which the hacker can then control. .[8]

Some Trojans take advantage of a security flaw in older versions of Internet Explorer and Google Chrome to use the host computer as an anonymizer proxy to effectively hide Internet usage,[9] enabling the controller to use the Internet for illegal purposes while all potentially incriminating evidence indicates the infected computer or its IP address. The host's computer may or may not show the internet history of the sites viewed using the computer as a proxy. The first generation of anonymizer Trojan horses tended to leave their tracks in the page view histories of the host computer. Later generations of the Trojan tend to "cover" their tracks more efficiently. Several versions of Sub7 have been widely circulated in the US and Europe and became the most widely distributed examples of this type of Trojan.[8]

In German-speaking countries, spyware used or made by the government is sometimes called *govware*. Govware is typically a Trojan software used to intercept communications from the target computer. Some countries like Switzerland and Germany have a legal framework governing the use of such software.[10] [11] Examples of govware trojans include the Swiss MiniPanzer and MegaPanzer[12] and the German "state trojan" nicknamed R2D2.[10]

Due to the popularity of botnets among hackers and the availability of advertising services that permit authors to violate their users' privacy, Trojans are becoming more common. According to a survey conducted by BitDefender from January to June 2009, "Trojan-type malware is on the rise, accounting for 83-percent of the global malware detected in the world." Trojans have a relationship with worms, as they spread with the help given by worms and travel across the internet with them.[13] BitDefender has stated that approximately 15% of computers are members of a botnet, usually recruited by a Trojan infection.[14]

Rootkit

A rootkit is a collection of computer software, typically malicious, designed to enable access to a computer or areas of its software that would not otherwise be allowed (for example, to an unauthorized user) and often masks its existence or the existence of other software.[1] The term *rootkit* is a concatenation of "root" (the traditional name of the privileged account on Unix-like operating systems) and the word "kit" (which refers to the software components that implement the tool). The term "rootkit" has negative connotations through its association with malware.[1]

Rootkit installation can be automated, or an attacker can install it once they've obtained root or Administrator access. Obtaining this access is a result of direct attack on a system, i.e. exploiting a known vulnerability (such as privilege escalation) or a password (obtained by cracking or social engineering tactics like "phishing"). Once installed, it becomes possible to hide the intrusion as well as to maintain privileged access. The key is the root or administrator access. Full control over a system means that existing software can be modified, including software that might otherwise be used to detect or circumvent it.

Rootkit detection is difficult because a rootkit may be able to subvert the software that is intended to find it. Detection methods include using an alternative and trusted operating system, behavioral-based methods, signature scanning, difference scanning, and memory dump analysis. Removal can be complicated or practically impossible, especially in cases where the rootkit resides in the kernel; reinstallation of the operating system may be the only available solution to the problem.[2] When dealing with firmware rootkits, removal may require hardware replacement, or specialized equipment.

Rootkit, History

The term *rootkit* or *root kit* originally referred to a maliciously modified set of administrative tools for a Unix-like operating system that granted "root" access.[3] If an intruder could replace the standard administrative tools on a system with a rootkit, the intruder could obtain root access over the system whilst simultaneously concealing these activities from the legitimate system administrator. These first-generation rootkits were trivial to detect by using tools such as Tripwire that had not been compromised to access the same information.[4][5] Lane Davis and Steven Dake wrote the earliest known rootkit in 1990 for Sun Microsystems' SunOS UNIX operating system.[6] In the lecture he gave upon receiving the Turing award in 1983, Ken Thompson of Bell Labs, one of the creators of Unix, theorized about subverting the C compiler in a Unix distribution and discussed the exploit. The modified compiler would detect attempts to compile the Unix `login` command and generate altered code that would accept not only the user's correct password, but an additional "backdoor" password known to the attacker. Additionally, the compiler would detect attempts to compile a new version of the compiler, and would insert the same exploits into the new compiler. A review of the source code for the `login` command or the updated compiler would not reveal any malicious code.[7] This exploit was equivalent to a rootkit.

The first documented computer virus to target the personal computer, discovered in 1986, used cloaking techniques to hide itself: the Brain virus intercepted attempts to read the boot sector, and redirected these to elsewhere on the disk, where a copy of the original boot sector was kept.[1] Over time, DOS-virus cloaking methods became more sophisticated, with advanced techniques including the hooking of low-level disk INT 13H BIOS interrupt calls to hide unauthorized modifications to files.[1]

The first malicious rootkit for the Windows NT operating system appeared in 1999: a trojan called *NTRootkit* created by Greg Hoglund.[8] It was followed by *HackerDefender* in 2003.[1] The first rootkit targeting Mac OS X appeared in 2009,[9] while the Stuxnet worm was the first to target programmable logic controllers (PLC).[10]

Rootkit, Uses

Modern rootkits do not elevate access,[3] but rather are used to make another software payload undetectable by adding stealth capabilities.[8] Most rootkits are classified as malware, because the payloads they are bundled with are malicious. For example, a payload might covertly steal user passwords, credit card information, computing resources, or conduct other unauthorized activities. A small number of rootkits may be considered utility applications by their users: for example, a rootkit might cloak a CD-ROM-emulation driver, allowing video game users to defeat anti-piracy measures that require insertion of the original installation media into a physical optical drive to verify that the software was legitimately purchased.

Rootkits and their payloads have many uses:

- Provide an attacker with full access via a backdoor, permitting unauthorized access to, for example, steal or falsify documents. One of the ways to carry this out is to subvert the login mechanism, such as the /bin/login program on Unix-like systems or GINA on Windows. The replacement appears to function normally, but also accepts a secret login combination that allows an attacker direct access to the system with administrative privileges, bypassing standard authentication and authorization mechanisms.

- Conceal other malware, notably password-stealing key loggers and computer viruses.[18]
- Appropriate the compromised machine as a zombie computer for attacks on other computers. (The attack originates from the compromised system or network, instead of the attacker's system.) "Zombie" computers are typically members of large botnets that can launch denial-of-service attacks, distribute e-mail spam, conduct click fraud, etc.
- Enforcement of digital rights management (DRM).

In some instances, rootkits provide desired functionality, and may be installed intentionally on behalf of the computer user:

- Conceal cheating in online games from software like Warden.[19]
- Detect attacks, for example, in a honeypot.[20]
- Enhance emulation software and security software.[21] Alcohol 120% and Daemon Tools are commercial examples of non-hostile rootkits used to defeat copy-protection mechanisms such as SafeDisc and SecuROM. Kaspersky antivirus software also uses techniques resembling rootkits to protect itself from malicious actions. It loads its own drivers to intercept system activity, and then prevents other processes from doing harm to itself. Its processes are not hidden, but cannot be terminated by standard methods (It can be terminated with Process Hacker).
- Anti-theft protection: Laptops may have BIOS-based rootkit software that will periodically report to a central authority, allowing the laptop to be monitored, disabled or wiped of information in the event that it is stolen.[22]
- Bypassing Microsoft Product Activation[23]

Rootkit, Types

There are at least five types of rootkit, ranging from those at the lowest level in firmware (with the highest privileges), through to the least privileged user-based variants that operate in Ring 3. Hybrid combinations of these may occur spanning, for example, user mode and kernel mode.[24]

Rootkit, Types, User Mode

User-mode rootkits run in Ring 3, along with other applications as user, rather than low-level system processes.[25] They have a number of possible installation vectors to intercept and modify the standard behavior of application programming interfaces (APIs). Some inject a dynamically linked library (such as a .DLL file on Windows, or a .dylib file on Mac OS X) into other processes, and are thereby able to execute inside any target process to spoof it; others with sufficient privileges simply overwrite the memory of a target application. Injection mechanisms include:[25]

- Use of vendor-supplied application extensions. For example, Windows Explorer has public interfaces that allow third parties to extend its functionality.
- Interception of messages.
- Debuggers.
- Exploitation of security vulnerabilities.
- Function hooking or patching of commonly used APIs, for example, to hide a running process or file that resides on a filesystem.[26]

...since user mode applications all run in their own memory space, the rootkit needs to perform this patching in the memory space of every running application. In addition, the rootkit needs to monitor the system for any new applications that execute and patch those programs' memory space before they fully execute.

— *Windows Rootkit Overview, Symantec[3]*

Rootkit, Types, Kernel Mode

Kernel-mode rootkits run with the highest operating system privileges (Ring 0) by adding code or replacing portions of the core operating system, including both the kernel and associated device drivers. Most operating systems support kernel-mode device drivers, which execute with the same privileges as the operating system itself. As such, many kernel-mode rootkits are developed as device drivers or loadable modules, such as loadable kernel modules in Linux or device drivers in Microsoft Windows. This class of rootkit has unrestricted security access, but is more difficult to write.[27] The complexity makes bugs common, and any bugs in code operating at the kernel level may seriously impact system stability, leading to discovery of the rootkit.[27] One of the first widely known kernel rootkits was developed for Windows NT 4.0 and released in Phrack magazine in 1999 by Greg Hoglund.[28][29][30] Kernel rootkits can be especially difficult to detect and remove because they operate at the same security level as the operating system itself, and are thus able to intercept or subvert the most trusted operating system operations. Any software, such as antivirus software, running on the compromised system is equally vulnerable.[31] In this situation, no part of the system can be trusted.

A rootkit can modify data structures in the Windows kernel using a method known as *direct kernel object manipulation* (DKOM).[32] This method can be used to hide processes. A kernel mode rootkit can also hook the System Service Descriptor Table (SSDT), or modify the gates between user mode and kernel mode, in order to cloak itself.[3] Similarly for the Linux operating system, a rootkit can modify the *system call table* to subvert kernel functionality.[33] It's common that a rootkit creates a hidden, encrypted filesystem in which it can hide other malware or original copies of files it has infected.[34] Operating systems are evolving to counter the threat of kernel-mode rootkits. For example, 64-bit editions of Microsoft Windows now implement mandatory signing of all kernel-level drivers in order to make it more difficult for untrusted code to execute with the highest privileges in a system.[35]

Rootkit, Types, Kernel Mode, Bootkits

A kernel-mode rootkit variant called a bootkit, it can infect startup code like the Master Boot Record (MBR), Volume Boot Record (VBR) or boot sector, and in this way, can be used to attack full disk encryption systems.

An example of such an attack on disk encryption is the "Evil Maid Attack", in which an attacker installs a bootkit on an unattended computer, replacing the legitimate boot loader with one under their control. Typically the malware loader persists through the transition to protected mode when the kernel has loaded, and is thus able to subvert the kernel.[36][37][38][39] For example, the "Stoned Bootkit" subverts the system by using a compromised boot loader to intercept encryption keys and passwords.[40] More recently, the Alureon rootkit has successfully subverted the requirement for 64-bit kernel-mode driver signing in Windows 7 by modifying the master boot record.[41] Although not malware in the sense of doing something the user doesn't want, certain "Vista Loader" or "Windows Loader" software works in a similar way by injecting an ACPI SLIC (System Licensed Internal Code) table in the RAM-cached version of the BIOS during boot, in order to defeat the Windows Vista and Windows 7 activation process.[42][43] This vector of attack was rendered useless in the (non-server) versions of Windows 8, which use a unique, machine-specific key for each system, that can only be used by that one machine.[44] Many antivirus companies provide free utilities and programs to remove bootkits.

Rootkit, Hypervisor Level

Rootkits have been created as Type II Hypervisors in academia as proofs of concept. By exploiting hardware virtualization features such as Intel VT or AMD-V, this type of rootkit runs in Ring -1 and hosts the target operating system as a virtual machine, thereby enabling the rootkit to intercept hardware calls made by the original operating system.[5] Unlike normal hypervisors, they do not have to load before the operating system, but can load into an operating system before promoting it into a virtual machine.[5] A hypervisor rootkit does not have to make any modifications to the kernel of the target to subvert it; however, that does not mean that it cannot be detected by the guest operating system. For example, timing differences may be detectable in CPU instructions.[5] The "SubVirt" laboratory rootkit, developed jointly by Microsoft and University of Michigan researchers, is an academic example of a virtual machine–based rootkit (VMBR),[45] while Blue Pill software is another. In 2009, researchers from Microsoft and North Carolina State University demonstrated a hypervisor-layer anti-rootkit called Hooksafe, which provides generic protection against kernel-mode rootkits.[46] Windows 10 introduced a new feature called "Device Guard", that takes advantage of virtualization to provide independent external protection of an operating system against rootkit-type malware.[47]

Rootkit, Firmware and Hardware

A firmware rootkit uses device or platform firmware to create a persistent malware image in hardware, such as a router, network card,[48] hard drive, or the system BIOS.[25][49] The rootkit hides in firmware, because firmware is not usually inspected for code integrity. John Heasman demonstrated the viability of firmware rootkits in both ACPI firmware routines[50] and in a PCI expansion card ROM.[51] In October 2008, criminals tampered with European credit card-reading machines before they were installed. The devices intercepted and transmitted credit card details via a mobile phone network.[52] In March 2009, researchers Alfredo Ortega and Anibal Sacco published details of a BIOS-level Windows rootkit that was able to survive disk replacement and operating system re-installation.[53][54][55] A few months later they learned that some laptops are sold with a legitimate rootkit, known as Absolute CompuTrace or Absolute LoJack for Laptops, preinstalled in many BIOS images. This is an anti-theft technology system that researchers showed can be turned to malicious purposes.[22]

Intel Active Management Technology, part of Intel vPro, implements out-of-band management, giving administrators remote administration, remote management, and remote control of PCs with no involvement of the host processor or BIOS, even when the system is powered off. Remote administration includes remote power-up and power-down, remote reset, redirected boot, console redirection, pre-boot access to BIOS settings, programmable filtering for inbound and outbound network traffic, agent presence checking, out-of-band policy-based alerting, access to system information, such as hardware asset information, persistent event logs, and other information that is stored in dedicated memory (not on the hard drive) where it is accessible even if the OS is down or the PC is powered off. Some of these functions require the deepest level of rootkit, a second non-removable spy computer built around the main computer. Sandy

Bridge and future chipsets have "the ability to remotely kill and restore a lost or stolen PC via 3G". Hardware rootkits built into the chipset can help recover stolen computers, remove data, or render them useless, but they also present privacy and security concerns of undetectable spying and redirection by management or hackers who might gain control.

Rootkit, Installation and Cloaking

Rootkits employ a variety of techniques to gain control of a system; the type of rootkit influences the choice of attack vector. The most common technique leverages security vulnerabilities to achieve surreptitious privilege escalation. Another approach is to use a Trojan horse, deceiving a computer user into trusting the rootkit's installation program as benign—in this case, social engineering convinces a user that the rootkit is beneficial.[27] The installation task is made easier if the principle of least privilege is not applied, since the rootkit then does not have to explicitly request elevated (administrator-level) privileges. Other classes of rootkits can be installed only by someone with physical access to the target system. Some rootkits may also be installed intentionally by the owner of the system or somebody authorized by the owner, e.g. for the purpose of employee monitoring, rendering such subversive techniques unnecessary.[56] The installation of malicious rootkits is commercially driven, with a pay-per-install (PPI) compensation method typical for distribution.[57][58]

Once installed, a rootkit takes active measures to obscure its presence within the host system through subversion or evasion of standard operating system security tools and application programming interface (APIs) used for diagnosis, scanning, and monitoring. Rootkits achieve this by modifying the behavior of core parts of an operating system through loading code into other processes, the installation or modification of drivers, or kernel modules. Obfuscation techniques include concealing running processes from system-monitoring mechanisms and hiding system files and other configuration data.[59] It is not uncommon for a rootkit to disable the event logging capacity of an operating system, in an attempt to hide evidence of an attack. Rootkits can, in theory, subvert *any* operating system activities.[60] The "perfect rootkit" can be thought of as similar to a "perfect crime": one that nobody realizes has taken place. Rootkits also take a number of measures to ensure their survival against detection and "cleaning" by antivirus software in addition to commonly installing into Ring 0 (kernel-mode), where they have complete access to a system. These include polymorphism (changing so their "signature" is hard to detect), stealth techniques, regeneration, disabling or turning off anti-malware software.[61] and not installing on virtual machines where it may be easier for researchers to discover and analyze them.

Rootkit, Detection

The fundamental problem with rootkit detection is that if the operating system has been subverted, particularly by a kernel-level rootkit, it cannot be trusted to find unauthorized modifications to itself or its components.[60] Actions such as requesting a list of running processes, or a list of files in a directory, cannot be trusted to behave as expected. In other words, rootkit detectors that work while running on infected systems are only effective against rootkits that have some defect in their camouflage, or that run with lower user-mode privileges than the detection software in the kernel.[27] As with computer viruses, the detection and elimination of rootkits is an ongoing struggle between both sides of this conflict.[60] Detection can take a number of different approaches, including looking for virus "signatures" (e.g. antivirus software), integrity checking (e.g. digital signatures), difference-based detection (comparison of expected vs. actual results), and behavioral detection (e.g. monitoring CPU usage or network traffic).

For kernel-mode rootkits, detection is considerably more complex, requiring careful scrutiny of the System Call Table to look for hooked functions where the malware may be subverting system behavior,[62] as well as forensic scanning of memory for patterns that indicate hidden processes. Unix rootkit detection offerings include Zeppoo,[63] chkrootkit, rkhunter and OSSEC. For Windows, detection tools include Microsoft Sysinternals RootkitRevealer,[64] Avast! Antivirus, Sophos Anti-Rootkit,[65] F-Secure,[66] Radix,[67] GMER,[68] and WindowsSCOPE. Any rootkit detectors that prove effective ultimately contribute to their own ineffectiveness, as malware authors adapt and test their code to escape detection by well-used tools. [Notes 1] Detection by examining storage while the suspect operating system is not operational can miss rootkits not recognised by the checking software, as the rootkit is not active and suspicious behavior is suppressed; conventional anti-malware software running with the rootkit operational may fail if the rootkit hides itself effectively.

Rootkit, Detection, Alternative Trusted Medium

The best and most reliable method for operating-system-level rootkit detection is to shut down the computer suspected of infection, and then to check its storage by booting from an alternative trusted medium (e.g. a "rescue" CD-ROM or USB flash drive).[69] The technique is effective because a rootkit cannot actively hide its presence if it is not running.

Rootkit, Detection, Behavioral-based

The behavioral-based approach to detecting rootkits attempts to infer the presence of a rootkit by looking for rootkit-like behavior. For example, by profiling a system, differences in the timing and frequency of API calls or in overall CPU utilization can be attributed to a rootkit. The method is complex and is hampered by a high incidence of false positives. Defective rootkits can sometimes introduce very obvious changes to a system: the Alureon rootkit crashed Windows systems after a security update exposed a design flaw in its code.[70][71] Logs from a packet analyzer, firewall, or intrusion prevention system may present evidence of rootkit behaviour in a networked environment.[24]

Rootkit, Detection, Signature-based

Antivirus products rarely catch all viruses in public tests (depending on what is used and to what extent), even though security software vendors incorporate rootkit detection into their products. Should a rootkit attempt to hide during an antivirus scan, a stealth detector may notice; if the rootkit attempts to temporarily unload itself from the system, signature detection (or "fingerprinting") can still find it. This combined approach forces attackers to implement counterattack mechanisms, or "retro" routines, that attempt to terminate antivirus programs. Signature-based detection methods can be effective against well-published rootkits, but less so against specially crafted, custom-root rootkits.[60]

Rootkit, Detection, Difference-based

Another method that can detect rootkits compares "trusted" raw data with "tainted" content returned by an API. For example, binaries present on disk can be compared with their copies within operating memory (in some operating systems, the in-memory image should be identical to the on-disk image), or the results returned from file system or Windows Registry APIs can be checked against raw structures on the underlying physical disks[60][72]—however, in the case of the former, some valid differences can be introduced by operating system mechanisms like memory relocation or shimming. A rootkit may detect the presence of a such difference-based scanner or virtual machine (the latter being commonly used to perform forensic analysis), and adjust its behaviour so that no differences can be detected. Difference-based detection was used by Russinovich's *RootkitRevealer* tool to find the Sony DRM rootkit.[1]

Rootkit, Detection, Integrity Checking

Code signing uses public-key infrastructure to check if a file has been modified since being digitally signed by its publisher. Alternatively, a system owner or administrator can use a cryptographic hash function to compute a "fingerprint" at installation time that can help to detect subsequent unauthorized changes to on-disk code libraries.[73] However, unsophisticated schemes check only whether the code has been modified since installation time; subversion prior to that time is not detectable. The fingerprint must be re-established each time changes are made to the system: for example, after installing security updates or a service pack. The hash function creates a *message digest*, a relatively short code calculated from each bit in the file using an algorithm that creates large changes in the message digest with even smaller changes to the original file. By recalculating and comparing the message digest of the installed files at regular intervals against a trusted list of message digests, changes in the system can be detected and monitored—as long as the original baseline was created before the malware was added.

More-sophisticated rootkits are able to subvert the verification process by presenting an unmodified copy of the file for inspection, or by making code modifications only in memory, rather than on disk. The technique may therefore be effective only against unsophisticated rootkits—for example, those that replace Unix binaries like "ls" to hide the presence of a file. Similarly, detection in firmware can be achieved by computing a cryptographic hash of the firmware and comparing it to a whitelist of expected values, or by extending the hash value into Trusted Platform Module (TPM) configuration registers, which are later compared to a whitelist of expected values.[74] The code that performs hash, compare, or extend operations must also be protected—in this context, the notion of an *immutable root-of-trust* holds that the very first code to measure security properties of a system must itself be trusted to ensure that a rootkit or bootkit does not compromise the system at its most fundamental level.[75]

Rootkit, Detection, Memory Dumps

Forcing a complete dump of virtual memory will capture an active rootkit (or a kernel dump in the case of a kernel-mode rootkit), allowing offline forensic analysis to be performed with a debugger against the resulting dump file, without the rootkit being able to take any measures to cloak itself. This technique is highly specialized, and may require access to non-public source code or debugging symbols. Memory dumps initiated by the operating system cannot always be used to detect a hypervisor-based rootkit, which is able to intercept and subvert the lowest-level attempts to read memory[5]—a hardware device, such as one that implements a non-maskable interrupt, may be required to dump memory in this scenario.[76][77] Virtual machines also make it easier to analyze the memory of a compromised machine from the underlying hypervisor, so some rootkits will avoid infecting virtual machines for this reason.

Rootkit, Removal

Manual removal of a rootkit is often too difficult for a typical computer user,[25] but a number of security-software vendors offer tools to automatically detect and remove some rootkits, typically as part of an antivirus suite. As of 2005, Microsoft's monthly Windows Malicious Software Removal Tool is able to detect and remove some classes of rootkits.[78][79] Also, Windows Defender Offline can remove rootkits, as it runs from a trusted environment before the operating system starts. Some antivirus scanners can bypass file system APIs, which are vulnerable to manipulation by a rootkit. Instead, they access raw filesystem structures directly, and use this information to validate the results from the system APIs to identify any differences that may be caused by a rootkit.[Notes 2][80][81][82][83] There are experts who believe that the only reliable way to remove them is to re-install the operating system from trusted media. [84][85] This is because antivirus and malware removal tools running on an untrusted system may be ineffective against well-written kernel-mode rootkits. Booting an alternative operating system from trusted media can allow an infected system volume to be mounted and potentially safely cleaned and critical data to be copied off—or, alternatively, a forensic examination performed.[24] Lightweight operating systems such as Windows PE, Windows Recovery Console, Windows Recovery Environment, BartPE, or Live Distros can be used for this purpose, allowing the system to be "cleaned". Even if the type and nature of a rootkit is known, manual repair may be impractical, while re-installing the operating system and applications is safer, simpler and quicker.[84]

Rootkit, Public Availability

Like much malware used by attackers, many rootkit implementations are shared and are easily available on the Internet. It is not uncommon to see a compromised system in which a sophisticated, publicly available rootkit hides the presence of unsophisticated worms or attack tools apparently written by inexperienced programmers.[24] Most of the rootkits available on the Internet originated as exploits or as academic "proofs of concept" to demonstrate varying methods of hiding things within a computer system and of taking unauthorized control of it.[86][*dubious – discuss*] Often not fully optimized for stealth, such rootkits sometimes leave unintended evidence of their presence. Even so, when such rootkits are used in an attack, they are often effective. Other rootkits with keylogging features such as GameGuard are installed as part of online commercial games.[*citation needed*]

Rootkit, Defenses

System hardening represents one of the first layers of defence against a rootkit, to prevent it from being able to install.[87] Applying security patches, implementing the principle of least privilege, reducing the attack surface and installing antivirus software are some standard security best practices that are effective against all classes of malware.[88] New secure boot specifications like Unified Extensible Firmware Interface have been designed to address the threat of bootkits, but even these are vulnerable if the security features they offer are not utilized.[49] For server systems, remote server attestation using technologies such as Intel Trusted Execution Technology (TXT) provide a way of validating that servers remain in a known good state. For example, Microsoft Bitlocker encrypting data-at-rest validates servers are in a known "good state" on bootup. PrivateCore vCage is a software offering that secures data-in-use (memory) to avoid bootkits and rootkits by validating servers are in a known "good" state on bootup. The PrivateCore implementation works in concert with Intel TXT and locks down server system interfaces to avoid potential bootkits and rootkits.

Man-in-the-middle Attack

In cryptography and computer security, a man-in-the-middle attack (MITM) is an attack where the attacker secretly relays and possibly alters the communication between two parties who believe they are directly communicating with each other. One example of man-in-the-2 attacks is active eavesdropping, in which the attacker makes independent connections with the victims and relays messages between them to make them believe they are talking directly to each other over a private connection, when in fact the entire conversation is controlled by the attacker. The attacker must be able to intercept all relevant messages passing between the two victims and inject new ones. This is straightforward in many circumstances; for example, an attacker within reception range of an unencrypted wireless access point (Wi-Fi) can insert himself as a man-in-the-middle.[1]

As an attack that aims at circumventing mutual authentication, or lack thereof, a man-in-the-middle attack can succeed only when the attacker can impersonate each endpoint to their satisfaction as expected from the legitimate ends. Most cryptographic protocols include some form of endpoint authentication specifically to prevent MITM attacks. For example, TLS can authenticate one or both parties using a mutually trusted certificate authority.[2]

Man-in-the-middle Attack, Example

Suppose Alice wishes to communicate with Bob. Meanwhile, Mallory wishes to intercept the conversation to eavesdrop and optionally to deliver a false message to Bob.

First, Alice asks Bob for his public key. If Bob sends his public key to Alice, but Mallory is able to intercept it, a man-in-the-middle attack can begin. Mallory sends a forged message to Alice that purports to come from Bob, but instead includes Mallory's public key.

Alice, believing this public key to be Bob's, encrypts her message with Mallory's key and sends the enciphered message back to Bob. Mallory again intercepts, deciphers the message using her private key, possibly alters it if she wants, and re-enciphers it using the public key Bob originally sent to Alice. When Bob receives the newly enciphered message, he believes it came from Alice.

1. Alice sends a message to Bob, which is intercepted by Mallory:

    Alice *"Hi Bob, it's Alice. Give me your key."* → Mallory   Bob

2. Mallory relays this message to Bob; Bob cannot tell it is not really from Alice:

    Alice   Mallory *"Hi Bob, it's Alice. Give me your key."* →   Bob

3. Bob responds with his encryption key:

    Alice   Mallory   ← *[Bob's key]* Bob

4. Mallory replaces Bob's key with her own, and relays this to Alice, claiming that it is Bob's key:

    Alice   ← *[Mallory's key]* Mallory   Bob

5. Alice encrypts a message with what she believes to be Bob's key, thinking that only Bob can read it:

> Alice *"Meet me at the bus stop!" [encrypted with Mallory's key]* →   Mallory   Bob

6. However, because it was actually encrypted with Mallory's key, Mallory can decrypt it, read it, modify it (if desired), re-encrypt with Bob's key, and forward it to Bob:

> Alice   Mallory *"Meet me at the van down by the river!" [encrypted with Bob's key]* → Bob

7. Bob thinks that this message is a secure communication from Alice.
8. Bob goes to the van down by the river and gets robbed by Mallory.
9. Alice does not know that Bob was robbed by Mallory thinking Bob is late.
10. Not seeing Bob for a while, she determines something happened to Bob.

This example[3][4][5] shows the need for Alice and Bob to have some way to ensure that they are truly each using each other's public keys, rather than the public key of an attacker. Otherwise, such attacks are generally possible, in principle, against any message sent using public-key technology. A variety of techniques can help defend against MITM attacks.

Man-in-the-middle Attack, Defense and Detection

MITM attacks can be prevented or by two means: authentication and tamper detection. Authentication provides some degree of certainty that a given message has come from a legitimate source. Tamper detection merely shows evidence that a message may have been altered.

Man-in-the-middle Attack, Defense and Detection, Authentication

All cryptographic systems that are secure against MITM attacks provide some method of authentication for messages. Most require an exchange of information (such as public keys) in addition to the message over a secure channel. Such protocols often use key-agreement protocols have been developed, with different security requirements for the secure channel, though some have attempted to remove the requirement for any secure channel at all.[6]

A public key infrastructure, such as Transport Layer Security, may harden Transmission Control Protocol against Man-in-the-middle-attacks. In such structures, clients and servers exchange certificates which are issued and verified by a trusted third party called a certificate authority (CA). If the original key to authenticate this CA has not been itself the subject of a MITM attack, then the certificates issued by the CA may be used to authenticate the messages sent by the owner of that certificate. Use of mutual authentication, in which both the server and the client validate the other's communication, covers both ends of a MITM attack, though the default behavior of most connections is to only authenticate the server.

Attestments, such as verbal communications of a shared value (as in ZRTP), or recorded attestments such as audio/visual recordings of a public key hash[7] are used to ward off MITM attacks, as visual media is much more difficult and time-consuming to imitate than simple data packet communication. However, these methods require a human in the loop in order to successfully initiate the transaction.

HTTP Public Key Pinning, sometimes called "certificate pinning", helps prevent a MITM attack in which the certificate authority itself is compromised, by having the server provide a list of "pinned" public key hashes during the first transaction. Subsequent transactions then require one or more of the keys in the list must be used by the server in order to authenticate that transaction.

DNSSEC extends the DNS protocol to use signatures to authenticate DNS records, preventing simple MITM attacks from directing a client to a malicious IP address.

Man-in-the-middle Attack, Defense and Detection, Tamper Detection

Latency examination can potentially detect the attack in certain situations,[8] such as with long calculations that lead into tens of seconds like hash functions. To detect potential attacks, parties check for discrepancies in response times. For example: Say that two parties normally take a certain amount of time to perform a particular transaction. If one transaction, however, were to take an abnormal length of time to reach the other party, this could be indicative of a third party's interference inserting additional latency in the transaction.

Quantum Cryptography, in theory, provides tamper-evidence for transactions through the no-cloning theorem. Protocols based on quantum cryptography typically authenticate part or all of their classical communication with an unconditionally secure authentication scheme e.g. Wegman-Carter authentication. [9]

Man-in-the-middle Attack, Defense and Detection, Forensic Analysis

Captured network traffic from what is suspected to be an attack can be analyzed in order to determine whether or not there was an attack and determine the source of the attack, if any. Important evidence to analyze when performing network forensics on a suspected attack includes:[10]

- IP address of the server
- DNS name of the server
- X.509 certificate of the server
  - Is the certificate self signed?
  - Is the certificate signed by a trusted CA?
  - Has the certificate been revoked?
  - Has the certificate been changed recently?
  - Do other clients, elsewhere on the Internet, also get the same certificate?

Denial-of-service Attack

In computing, a denial-of-service attack (DoS attack) is a cyber-attack where the perpetrator seeks to make a machine or network resource unavailable to its intended users by temporarily or indefinitely disrupting services of a host connected to the Internet. Denial of service is typically accomplished by flooding the targeted machine or resource with superfluous requests in an attempt to overload systems and prevent some or all legitimate requests from being fulfilled.[1]

In a distributed denial-of-service attack (DDoS attack), the incoming traffic flooding the victim originates from many different sources. This effectively makes it impossible to stop the attack simply by blocking a single source.

A DoS or DDoS attack is analogous to a group of people crowding the entry door or gate to a shop or business, and not letting legitimate parties enter into the shop or business, disrupting normal operations.

Criminal perpetrators of DoS attacks often target sites or services hosted on high-profile web servers such as banks or credit card payment gateways. Revenge, blackmail[2][3][4] and activism[5] can motivate these attacks.

Denial-of-service Attack, History

Court testimony shows that the first demonstration of DoS attack was made by Khan C. Smith in 1997 during a DEF CON event disrupting Internet access to the Las Vegas Strip for over an hour and the release of sample code during the event led to the online attack of Sprint, EarthLink, E-Trade, and other major corporations in the year to follow.[6]

Denial-of-service Attack, Types

Denial-of-service attacks are characterized by an explicit attempt by attackers to prevent legitimate users of a service from using that service. In a distributed denial-of-service (DDoS) attack, the incoming traffic flooding the victim originates from many different sources – potentially hundreds of thousands or more. This effectively makes it impossible to stop the attack simply by blocking a single IP address; plus, it is very difficult to distinguish legitimate user traffic from attack traffic when spread across so many points of origin. There are two general forms of DoS attacks: those that crash services and those that flood services. The most serious attacks are distributed.[7] Many attacks involve forging of IP sender addresses (IP address spoofing) so that the location of the attacking machines cannot easily be identified and so that the attack cannot be easily defeated using ingress filtering.

Denial-of-service Attack, Types, Distributed DoS

A distributed denial-of-service (DDoS) is a cyber-attack where the perpetrator uses more than one unique IP address, often thousands of them. The scale of DDoS attacks has continued to rise over recent years, by 2016 exceeding a terabit per second.[8] [9]

Denial-of-service Attack, Types, Application Layer Attacks

An application layer DDoS attack (sometimes referred to as layer 7 DDoS attack) is a form of DDoS attack where attackers target the application layer of the OSI model.[10][11] The attack over-exercises specific functions or features of a website with the intention to disable those functions or features. This application-layer attack is different from an entire network attack, and is often used against financial institutions to distract IT and security personnel from security breaches.[12] As of 2013, application layer DDoS attacks represent 20% of all DDoS attacks.[13] According to research by the company Akamai, there have been "51 percent more application layer attacks" from Q4 2013 to Q4 2014 and "16 percent more" from Q3 2014 over Q4 2014.[14]

Denial-of-service Attack, Types, Application Layer Attacks, Application Layer

The Open Systems Interconnection (OSI) model (ISO/IEC 7498-1) is a conceptual model that characterizes and standardizes the internal functions of a communication system by partitioning it into abstraction layers. The model is a product of the Open Systems Interconnection project at the International Organization for Standardization (ISO). The model groups similar communication functions into one of seven logical layers. A layer serves the layer above it and is served by the layer below it. For example, a layer that provides error-free communications across a network provides the path needed by applications above it, while it calls the next lower layer to send and receive packets that make up the contents of that path. Two instances at one layer are connected by a horizontal connection on that layer.

In the OSI model, the definition of its application layer is narrower in scope. The OSI model defines the application layer as being the user interface. The OSI application layer is responsible for displaying data and images to the user in a human-recognizable format and to interface with the presentation layer below it.

Denial-of-service Attack, Types, Application Layer Attacks, Method of Attack

An application layer DDoS attack is done mainly for specific targeted purposes, including disrupting transactions and access to databases. It requires less resources and often accompanies network layer attacks.[15] An attack is disguised to look like legitimate traffic, except it targets specific application packets.[13] The attack on the application layer can disrupt services such as the retrieval of information or search function[13] as well as web browser function, email services and photo applications. In order to be deemed a *distributed* denial of service attack, more than around 3–5 nodes on different networks should be used; using fewer than 3–5 nodes qualifies as a Denial-of-service attack and not a DdoS.[11][16]

Denial-of-service Attack, Types, Application Layer Attacks, Defending Application Layer DDoS Attacks

Defending against an application layer DDoS attack requires DDoS mitigation. Success of mitigation requires correctly identifying incoming traffic to separate human traffic from human-like bots and hijacked browsers.

Denial-of-service Attack, Types, Advanced Persistent DoS

An advanced persistent DoS (APDoS) is more likely to be perpetrated by an advanced persistent threat (APT): actors who are well-resourced, exceptionally skilled and have access to substantial commercial grade computer resources and capacity. APDoS attacks represent a clear and emerging threat needing specialised monitoring and incident response services and the defensive capabilities of specialised DDoS mitigation service providers.

This type of attack involves massive network layer DDoS attacks through to focused application layer (HTTP) floods, followed by repeated (at varying intervals) SQLi and XSS attacks.[17][*citation needed*] Typically, the perpetrators can simultaneously use from 2 to 5 attack vectors involving up to several tens of millions of requests per second, often accompanied by large SYN floods that can not only attack the victim but also any service provider implementing any sort of managed DDoS mitigation capability. These attacks can persist for several weeks- the longest continuous period noted so far lasted 38 days. This APDoS attack involved approximately 50+ petabits (50,000+ terabits) of malicious traffic.

Attackers in this scenario may (or often will) tactically switch between several targets to create a diversion to evade defensive DDoS countermeasures but all the while eventually concentrating the main thrust of the attack onto a single victim. In this scenario, threat actors with continuous access to several very powerful network resources are capable of sustaining a prolonged campaign generating enormous levels of un-amplified DDoS traffic.

APDoS attacks are characterised by:

- advanced reconnaissance (pre-attack OSINT and extensive decoyed scanning crafted to evade detection over long periods)
- tactical execution (attack with a primary and secondary victims but focus is on primary)
- explicit motivation (a calculated end game/goal target)
- large computing capacity (access to substantial computer power and network bandwidth resources)
- simultaneous multi-threaded OSI layer attacks (sophisticated tools operating at layers 3 through 7)
- persistence over extended periods (utilising all the above into a concerted, well managed attack across a range of targets[18]).

Denial-of-service Attack, Types, Denial-of-service as a Service

Some vendors provide so-called "booter" or "stresser" services, which have simple web-based front ends, and accept payment over the web. Marketed and promoted as stress-testing tools, they can be used to perform unauthorized denial-of-service attacks, and allow technically unsophisticated attackers access to sophisticated attack tools without the need for the attacker to understand their use.[19]

Denial-of-service Attack, Symptoms

The United States Computer Emergency Readiness Team (US-CERT) has identified symptoms of a denial-of-service attack to include:[20]

- unusually slow network performance (opening files or accessing web sites)
- unavailability of a particular web site
- inability to access any web site
- dramatic increase in the number of spam emails received (this type of DoS attack is considered an e-mail bomb).

Additional symptoms may include:

- disconnection of a wireless or wired internet connection
- long-term denial of access to the web or any internet services.

If the attack is conducted on a sufficiently large scale, entire geographical regions of Internet connectivity can be compromised without the attacker's knowledge or intent by incorrectly configured or flimsy network infrastructure equipment.

Denial-of-service Attack, Attack Techniques

A wide array of programs are used to launch DoS-attacks.

Denial-of-service Attack, Attack Techniques, Attack Tools

In cases such as MyDoom the tools are embedded in malware, and launch their attacks without the knowledge of the system owner. Stacheldraht is a classic example of a DDoS tool. It utilizes a layered structure where the attacker uses a client program to connect to handlers, which are compromised systems that issue commands to the zombie agents, which in turn facilitate the DDoS attack. Agents are compromised via the handlers by the attacker, using automated routines to exploit vulnerabilities in programs that accept remote connections running on the targeted remote hosts. Each handler can control up to a thousand agents.[21]

In other cases a machine may become part of a DDoS attack with the owner's consent, for example, in Operation Payback, organized by the group Anonymous. The LOIC has typically been used in this way. Along with HOIC a wide variety of DDoS tools are available today, including paid and free versions, with different features available. There is an underground market for these in hacker related forums and IRC channels.

UK's GCHQ has tools built for DDoS, named PREDATORS FACE and ROLLING THUNDER.[22]

Denial-of-service Attack, Attack Techniques, Application-layer Floods

Various DoS-causing exploits such as buffer overflow can cause server-running software to get confused and fill the disk space or consume all available memory or CPU time.

Other kinds of DoS rely primarily on brute force, flooding the target with an overwhelming flux of packets, oversaturating its connection bandwidth or depleting the target's system resources. Bandwidth-saturating floods rely on the attacker having higher bandwidth available than the victim; a common way of achieving this today is via distributed denial-of-service, employing a botnet. Another target of DDoS attacks may be to produce added costs for the application operator, when the latter uses resources based on Cloud Computing. In this case normally application used resources are tied to a needed Quality of Service level (e.g. responses should be less than 200 ms) and this rule is usually linked to automated software (e.g. Amazon CloudWatch[23]) to raise more virtual resources from the provider in order to meet the defined QoS levels for the increased requests.The main incentive behind such attacks may be to drive the application owner to raise the elasticity levels in order to handle the increased application traffic, in order to cause financial losses or force them to become less competitive. Other floods may use specific packet types or connection requests to saturate finite resources by, for example, occupying the maximum number of open connections or filling the victim's disk space with logs.

A "banana attack" is another particular type of DoS. It involves redirecting outgoing messages from the client back onto the client, preventing outside access, as well as flooding the client with the sent packets. A LAND attack is of this type.

An attacker with shell-level access to a victim's computer may slow it until it is unusable or crash it by using a fork bomb.

A kind of application-level DoS attack is XDoS (or XML DoS) which can be controlled by modern web application firewalls (WAFs).

Denial-of-service Attack, Attack Techniques, Degradation-of-service Attacks

"Pulsing" zombies are compromised computers that are directed to launch intermittent and short-lived floodings of victim websites with the intent of merely slowing it rather than crashing it. This type of attack, referred to as "degradation-of-service" rather than "denial-of-service", can be more difficult to detect than regular zombie invasions and can disrupt and hamper connection to websites for prolonged periods of time, potentially causing more disruption than concentrated floods.[24][25] Exposure of degradation-of-service attacks is complicated further by the matter of discerning whether the server is really being attacked or under normal traffic loads.[26]

Denial-of-service Attack, Attack Techniques, Denial-of-service Level II

The goal of DoS L2 (possibly DDoS) attack is to cause a launching of a defense mechanism which blocks the network segment from which the attack originated. In case of distributed attack or IP header modification (that depends on the kind of security behavior) it will fully block the attacked network from the Internet, but without system crash.[17][*citation needed*]

Denial-of-service Attack, Attack Techniques, Distributed DoS Attack

A distributed denial-of-service (DDoS) attack occurs when multiple systems flood the bandwidth or resources of a targeted system, usually one or more web servers.[7] Such an attack is often the result of multiple compromised systems (for example, a botnet) flooding the targeted system with traffic. A botnet is a network of zombie computers programmed to receive commands without the owners' knowledge.[27] When a server is overloaded with connections, new connections can no longer be accepted. The major advantages to an attacker of using a distributed denial-of-service attack are that multiple machines can generate more attack traffic than one machine, multiple attack machines are harder to turn off than one attack machine, and that the behavior of each attack machine can be stealthier, making it harder to track and shut down. These attacker advantages cause challenges for defense mechanisms. For example, merely purchasing more incoming bandwidth than the current volume of the attack might not help, because the attacker might be able to simply add more attack machines. This, after all, will end up completely crashing a website for periods of time.

Malware can carry DDoS attack mechanisms; one of the better-known examples of this was MyDoom. Its DoS mechanism was triggered on a specific date and time. This type of DDoS involved hardcoding the target IP address prior to release of the malware and no further interaction was necessary to launch the attack.

A system may also be compromised with a trojan, allowing the attacker to download a zombie agent, or the trojan may contain one. Attackers can also break into systems using automated tools that exploit flaws in programs that listen for connections from remote hosts. This scenario primarily concerns systems acting as servers on the web. Stacheldraht is a classic example of a DDoS tool. It utilizes a layered structure where the attacker uses a client program to connect to handlers, which are compromised systems that issue commands to the zombie agents, which in turn facilitate the DDoS attack. Agents are compromised via the handlers by the attacker, using automated routines to exploit vulnerabilities in programs that accept remote connections running on the targeted remote hosts. Each handler can control up to a thousand agents.[21] In some cases a machine may become part of a DDoS attack with the owner's consent, for example, in Operation Payback, organized by the group Anonymous. These attacks can use different types of internet packets such as: TCP, UDP, ICMP etc.

These collections of systems compromisers are known as botnets / rootservers. DDoS tools like Stacheldraht still use classic DoS attack methods centered on IP spoofing and amplification like smurf attacks and fraggle attacks (these are also known as bandwidth consumption attacks). SYN floods (also known as resource starvation attacks) may also be used. Newer tools can use DNS servers for DoS purposes. Unlike MyDoom's DDoS mechanism, botnets can be turned against any IP address. Script kiddies use them to deny the availability of well known websites to legitimate users.[28] More sophisticated attackers use DDoS tools for the purposes of extortion – even against their business rivals. [29]

Simple attacks such as SYN floods may appear with a wide range of source IP addresses, giving the appearance of a well distributed DoS. These flood attacks do not require completion of the TCP three way handshake and attempt to exhaust the destination SYN queue or the server bandwidth. Because the source IP addresses can be trivially spoofed, an attack could come from a limited set of sources, or may even originate from a single host. Stack enhancements such as syn cookies may be effective mitigation against SYN queue flooding, however complete bandwidth exhaustion may require involvement.[*further explanation needed*]

If an attacker mounts an attack from a single host it would be classified as a DoS attack. In fact, any attack against availability would be classed as a denial-of-service attack. On the other hand, if an attacker uses many systems to simultaneously launch attacks against a remote host, this would be classified as a DDoS attack.

It has been reported that there are new attacks from internet of things which have been involved in denial of service attacks. [30] In one noted attack that was made peaked at around 20,000 requests per second which came from around 900 CCTV cameras. [31]

UK's GCHQ has tools built for DDoS, named PREDATORS FACE and ROLLING THUNDER.[22]

Denial-of-service Attack, Attack Techniques, DDoS Extortion

In 2015, DDoS botnets such as DD4BC grew in prominence, taking aim at financial institutions.[32] Cyber-extortionists typically begin with a low-level attack and a warning that a larger attack will be carried out if a ransom is not paid in Bitcoin.[33] Security experts recommend targeted websites to not pay the ransom. The attackers tend to get into an extended extortion scheme once they recognize that the target is ready to pay.[34]

Denial-of-service Attack, Attack Techniques, HTTP POST DoS Attack

First discovered in 2009, the HTTP POST attack sends a complete, legitimate HTTP POST header, which includes a 'Content-Length' field to specify the size of the message body to follow. However, the attacker then proceeds to send the actual message body at an extremely slow rate (e.g. 1 byte/110 seconds). Due to the entire message being correct and complete, the target server will attempt to obey the 'Content-Length' field in the header, and wait for the entire body of the message to be transmitted, which can take a very long time. The attacker establishes hundreds or even thousands of such connections, until all resources for incoming connections on the server (the victim) are used up, hence making any further (including legitimate) connections impossible until all data has been sent. It is notable that unlike many other (D)DoS attacks, which try to subdue the server by overloading its network or CPU, a HTTP POST attack targets the *logical* resources of the victim, which means the victim would still have enough network bandwidth and processing power to operate.[35] Further combined with the fact that Apache will, by default, accept requests up to 2GB in size, this attack can be particularly powerful. HTTP POST attacks are difficult to differentiate from legitimate connections, and are therefore able to bypass some protection systems. OWASP, an open source web application security project, has released a testing tool to test the security of servers against this type of attacks.

Denial-of-service Attack, Attack Techniques, Internet Control Message Protocol (ICMP) Flood

A smurf attack relies on misconfigured network devices that allow packets to be sent to all computer hosts on a particular network via the broadcast address of the network, rather than a specific machine. The attacker will send large numbers of IP packets with the source address faked to appear to be the address of the victim. The network's bandwidth is quickly used up, preventing legitimate packets from getting through to their destination.[36]

Ping flood is based on sending the victim an overwhelming number of ping packets, usually using the "ping" command from Unix-like hosts (the -t flag on Windows systems is much less capable of overwhelming a target, also the -l (size) flag does not allow sent packet size greater than 65500 in Windows). It is very simple to launch, the primary requirement being access to greater bandwidth than the victim.

Ping of death is based on sending the victim a malformed ping packet, which will lead to a system crash on a vulnerable system.

The BlackNurse attack is an example of an attack taking advantage of the required Destination Port

Unreachable ICMP packets.

Denial-of-service Attack, Attack Techniques, Nuke

A Nuke is an old denial-of-service attack against computer networks consisting of fragmented or otherwise invalid ICMP packets sent to the target, achieved by using a modified ping utility to repeatedly send this corrupt data, thus slowing down the affected computer until it comes to a complete stop.

A specific example of a nuke attack that gained some prominence is the WinNuke, which exploited the vulnerability in the NetBIOS handler in Windows 95. A string of out-of-band data was sent to TCP port 139 of the victim's machine, causing it to lock up and display a Blue Screen of Death (BSOD).

Denial-of-service Attack, Attack Techniques, Peer-to-peer Attacks

Attackers have found a way to exploit a number of bugs in peer-to-peer servers to initiate DDoS attacks. The most aggressive of these peer-to-peer-DDoS attacks exploits DC++. With peer-to-peer there is no botnet and the attacker does not have to communicate with the clients it subverts. Instead, the attacker acts as a "puppet master," instructing clients of large peer-to-peer file sharing hubs to disconnect from their peer-to-peer network and to connect to the victim's website instead.[37][38][39]

Denial-of-service Attack, Attack Techniques, Permanent Denial-of-service Attacks

Permanent denial-of-service (PDoS), also known loosely as phlashing,[40] is an attack that damages a system so badly that it requires replacement or reinstallation of hardware.[41] Unlike the distributed denial-of-service attack, a PDoS attack exploits security flaws which allow remote administration on the management interfaces of the victim's hardware, such as routers, printers, or other networking hardware. The attacker uses these vulnerabilities to replace a device's firmware with a modified, corrupt, or defective firmware image—a process which when done legitimately is known as *flashing*. This therefore "bricks" the device, rendering it unusable for its original purpose until it can be repaired or replaced.

The PDoS is a pure hardware targeted attack which can be much faster and requires fewer resources than using a botnet or a root/vserver in a DDoS attack. Because of these features, and the potential and high probability of security exploits on Network Enabled Embedded Devices (NEEDs), this technique has come to the attention of numerous hacking communities.

PhlashDance is a tool created by Rich Smith (an employee of Hewlett-Packard's Systems Security Lab) used to detect and demonstrate PDoS vulnerabilities at the 2008 EUSecWest Applied Security Conference in London.[42]

Denial-of-service Attack, Attack Techniques, Reflected / Spoofed Attack

A distributed denial-of-service attack may involve sending forged requests of some type to a very large number of computers that will reply to the requests. Using Internet Protocol address spoofing, the source address is set to that of the targeted victim, which means all the replies will go to (and flood) the target. (This reflected attack form is sometimes called a "DRDOS".[43])

ICMP Echo Request attacks (Smurf attack) can be considered one form of reflected attack, as the flooding host(s) send Echo Requests to the broadcast addresses of mis-configured networks, thereby enticing hosts to send Echo Reply packets to the victim. Some early DDoS programs implemented a distributed form of this attack.

Denial-of-service Attack, Attack Techniques, Amplification

Amplification attacks are used to magnify the bandwidth that is sent to a victim. This is typically done through publicly accessible DNS servers that are used to cause congestion on the target system using DNS response traffic. Many services can be exploited to act as reflectors, some harder to block than others.[44] US-CERT have observed that different services implies in different amplification factors, as you can see below:[45]

UDP-based Amplification Attacks

Protocol	Bandwidth Amplification Factor
NTP	556.9
CharGen	358.8
DNS	up to 179 [46]
QOTD	140.3
Quake Network Protocol	63.9
BitTorrent	4.0 - 54.3 [47]
SSDP	30.8
Kad	16.3
SNMPv2	6.3
Steam Protocol	5.5
NetBIOS	3.8

DNS amplification attacks involve a new mechanism that increased the amplification effect, using a much larger list of DNS servers than seen earlier. The process typically involves an attacker sending a DNS name look up request to a public DNS server, spoofing the source IP address of the targeted victim. The attacker tries to request as much zone information as possible, thus amplifying the DNS record response that is sent to the targeted victim. Since the size of the request is significantly smaller than the response, the attacker is easily able to increase the amount of traffic directed at the target.[48][49] SNMP and NTP can also be exploited as reflector in an amplification attack.

An example of an amplified DDoS attack through NTP is through a command called monlist, which sends the details of the last 600 people who have requested the time from that computer back to the requester. A small request to this time server can be sent using a spoofed source IP address of some victim, which results in 556.9 times the amount of data that was requested back to the victim. This becomes amplified when using botnets that all send requests with the same spoofed IP source, which will send a massive amount of data back to the victim.

It is very difficult to defend against these types of attacks because the response data is coming from legitimate servers. These attack requests are also sent through UDP, which does not require a connection to the server. This means that the source IP is not verified when a request is received by the server. In order to bring awareness of these vulnerabilities, campaigns have been started that are dedicated to finding amplification vectors which has led to people fixing their resolvers or having the resolvers shut down completely.

Denial-of-service Attack, Attack Techniques, R-U-Dead-Yet? (RUDY)

RUDY attack targets web applications by starvation of available sessions on the web server. Much like Slowloris, RUDY keeps sessions at halt using never-ending POST transmissions and sending an arbitrarily large content-length header value.

Denial-of-service Attack, Attack Techniques, Shrew Attack

The shrew attack is a denial-of-service attack on the Transmission Control Protocol. It uses short synchronized bursts of traffic to disrupt TCP connections on the same link, by exploiting a weakness in TCP's retransmission timeout mechanism.[50]

Denial-of-service Attack, Attack Techniques, Slow Read Attack

A slow read attack sends legitimate application layer requests, but reads responses very slowly, thus trying to exhaust the server's connection pool. It is achieved by advertising a very small number for the TCP Receive Window size, and at the same time emptying clients' TCP receive buffer slowly, which causes a very low data flow rate.

Denial-of-service Attack, Attack Techniques, Sophisticated Low-bandwidth Distributed Denial-of-Service Attack

A sophisticated low-bandwidth DDoS attack is a form of DoS that uses less traffic and increases their effectiveness by aiming at a weak point in the victim's system design, i.e., the attacker sends traffic consisting of complicated requests to the system.[51] Essentially, a sophisticated DDoS attack is lower in cost due to its use of less traffic, is smaller in size making it more difficult to identify, and it has the ability to hurt systems which are protected by flow control mechanisms.[51][52]

Denial-of-service Attack, Attack Techniques, (S)SYN Flood

A SYN flood occurs when a host sends a flood of TCP/SYN packets, often with a forged sender address. Each of these packets are handled like a connection request, causing the server to spawn a half-open connection, by sending back a TCP/SYN-ACK packet (Acknowledge), and waiting for a packet in response from the sender address (response to the ACK Packet). However, because the sender address is forged, the response never comes. These half-open connections saturate the number of available connections the server can make, keeping it from responding to legitimate requests until after the attack ends.[53]

Denial-of-service Attack, Attack Techniques, Teardrop Attacks

A teardrop attack involves sending mangled IP fragments with overlapping, oversized payloads to the target machine. This can crash various operating systems because of a bug in their TCP/IP fragmentation re-assembly code.[54] Windows 3.1x, Windows 95 and Windows NT operating systems, as well as versions of Linux prior to versions 2.0.32 and 2.1.63 are vulnerable to this attack.

(Although in September 2009, a vulnerability in Windows Vista was referred to as a "teardrop attack", this targeted SMB2 which is a higher layer than the TCP packets that teardrop used).[55][56]

One of the fields in an IP header is the "fragment offset" field, indicating the starting position, or offset, of the data contained in a fragmented packet relative to the data in the original packet. If the sum of the offset and size of one fragmented packet differs from that of the next fragmented packet, the packets overlap. When this happens, a server vulnerable to teardrop attacks is unable to reassemble the packets - resulting in a denial-of-service condition.

Denial-of-service Attack, Attack Techniques, Telephony Denial-of-service (TDoS)

Voice over IP has made abusive origination of large numbers of telephone voice calls inexpensive and readily automated while permitting call origins to be misrepresented through caller ID spoofing.

According to the US Federal Bureau of Investigation, telephony denial-of-service (TDoS) has appeared as part of various fraudulent schemes:

- A scammer contacts the victim's banker or broker, impersonating the victim to request a funds transfer. The banker's attempt to contact the victim for verification of the transfer fails as the victim's telephone lines are being flooded with thousands of bogus calls, rendering the victim unreachable.[57]
- A scammer contacts consumers with a bogus claim to collect an outstanding payday loan for thousands of dollars. When the consumer objects, the scammer retaliates by flooding the victim's employer with thousands of automated calls. In some cases, displayed caller ID is spoofed to impersonate police or law enforcement agencies.[58]
- A scammer contacts consumers with a bogus debt collection demand and threatens to send police; when the victim balks, the scammer floods local police numbers with calls on which caller ID is spoofed to display the victims number. Police soon arrive at the victim's residence attempting to find the origin of the calls.

Telephony denial-of-service can exist even without Internet telephony. In the 2002 New Hampshire Senate election phone jamming scandal, telemarketers were used to flood political opponents with spurious calls to jam phone banks on election day. Widespread publication of a number can also flood it with enough calls to render it unusable, as happened by accident in 1981 with multiple +1-area code-867-5309 subscribers inundated by hundreds of misdialed calls daily in response to the song 867-5309/Jenny.

TDoS differs from other telephone harassment (such as prank calls and obscene phone calls) by the number of calls originated; by occupying lines continuously with repeated automated calls, the victim is prevented from making or receiving both routine and emergency telephone calls.

Related exploits include SMS flooding attacks and black fax or fax loop transmission.

Denial-of-service Attack, Defense Techniques

Defensive responses to denial-of-service attacks typically involve the use of a combination of attack detection, traffic classification and response tools, aiming to block traffic that they identify as illegitimate and allow traffic that they identify as legitimate.[59] A list of prevention and response tools is provided below:

Denial-of-service Attack, Defense Techniques, Application Front End Hardware

Application front-end hardware is intelligent hardware placed on the network before traffic reaches the servers. It can be used on networks in conjunction with routers and switches. Application front end hardware analyzes data packets as they enter the system, and then identifies them as priority, regular, or dangerous. There are more than 25 bandwidth management vendors.

Denial-of-service Attack, Defense Techniques, Application Level Key Completion Indicators

In order to meet the case of application level DDoS attacks against cloud-based applications, approaches may be based on an application layer analysis, to indicate whether an incoming traffic bulk is legitimate or not and thus enable the triggering of elasticity decisions without the economical implications of a DDoS attack.[60] These approaches mainly rely on an identified path of value inside the application and monitor the macroscopic progress of the requests in this path, towards the final generation of profit, through markers denoted as Key Completion Indicators.[61]

In essence, this technique is a statistical method of assessing the behavior of incoming requests to detect if something unusual or abnormal is going on. Imagine if you were to observe the behavior of normal, paying customers at a brick-and-mortar department store. On average, they would spend in aggregate a known percentage of time on different activities such as picking up items and examining them, putting them back on shelves, trying on clothes, filling a basket, waiting in line, paying for their purchases, and leaving. These high-level activities correspond to the Key Completion Indicators in a service or site, and once normal behavior is determined, abnormal behavior can be identified. For example, if a huge number of customers arrive and spend all their time picking up items and setting them down, but never making any purchases, this can be flagged as unusual behavior.

In the case of elastic cloud services where a huge and abnormal additional workload may incur significant charges from the cloud service provider, this technique can be used to stop or even scale back the elastic expansion of server availability in order to protect from economic loss. In the example analogy, imagine that the department store had the ability to bring in additional employees on a few minutes' notice and routinely did this during "rushes" of unusual customer volume. If a mob shows up that never does any buying, after a relatively short time of paying for the additional employee costs, the store can scale back the number of employees, understanding that the non-buying customers provide no profit for the store and thus should not be serviced. While this may prevent the store from making sales to legitimate customers during the period of attack, it saves the potentially ruinous cost of calling up huge numbers of employees to service an illegitimate load.

Denial-of-service Attack, Defense Techniques, Blackholing and Sinkholing

With blackhole routing, all the traffic to the attacked DNS or IP address is sent to a "black hole" (null interface or a non-existent server). To be more efficient and avoid affecting network connectivity, it can be managed by the ISP.[62]

A DNS sinkhole routes traffic to a valid IP address which analyzes traffic and rejects bad packets. Sinkholing is not efficient for most severe attacks.

Denial-of-service Attack, Defense Techniques, IPS Based Prevention

Intrusion prevention systems (IPS) are effective if the attacks have signatures associated with them. However, the trend among the attacks is to have legitimate content but bad intent. Intrusion-prevention systems which work on content recognition cannot block behavior-based DoS attacks.[17][*citation needed*]

An ASIC based IPS may detect and block denial-of-service attacks because they have the processing power and the granularity to analyze the attacks and act like a circuit breaker in an automated way.[17][*citation needed*]

A rate-based IPS (RBIPS) must analyze traffic granularly and continuously monitor the traffic pattern and determine if there is traffic anomaly. It must let the legitimate traffic flow while blocking the DoS attack traffic.[63]

Denial-of-service Attack, Defense Techniques, DDS Based Defense

More focused on the problem than IPS, a DoS defense system (DDS) can block connection-based DoS attacks and those with legitimate content but bad intent. A DDS can also address both protocol attacks (such as teardrop and ping of death) and rate-based attacks (such as ICMP floods and SYN floods).

Denial-of-service Attack, Defense Techniques, Firewalls

In the case of a simple attack, a firewall could have a simple rule added to deny all incoming traffic from the attackers, based on protocols, ports or the originating IP addresses.

More complex attacks will however be hard to block with simple rules: for example, if there is an ongoing attack on port 80 (web service), it is not possible to drop all incoming traffic on this port because doing so will prevent the server from serving legitimate traffic.[64] Additionally, firewalls may be too deep in the network hierarchy, with routers being adversely affected before the traffic gets to the firewall.

Denial-of-service Attack, Defense Techniques, Routers

Similar to switches, routers have some rate-limiting and ACL capability. They, too, are manually set. Most routers can be easily overwhelmed under a DoS attack. Cisco IOS has optional features that can reduce the impact of flooding.[65]

Denial-of-service Attack, Defense Techniques, Switches

Most switches have some rate-limiting and ACL capability. Some switches provide automatic and/or system-wide rate limiting, traffic shaping, delayed binding (TCP splicing), deep packet inspection and Bogon filtering (bogus IP filtering) to detect and remediate DoS attacks through automatic rate filtering and WAN Link failover and balancing.[17][*citation needed*]

These schemes will work as long as the DoS attacks can be prevented by using them. For example, SYN flood can be prevented using delayed binding or TCP splicing. Similarly content based DoS may be prevented using deep packet inspection. Attacks originating from dark addresses or going to dark addresses can be prevented using bogon filtering. Automatic rate filtering can work as long as set rate-thresholds have been set correctly. Wan-link failover will work as long as both links have DoS/DDoS prevention mechanism.[17][*citation needed*]

Denial-of-service Attack, Defense Techniques, Upstream Filtering

All traffic is passed through a "cleaning center" or a "scrubbing center" via various methods such as proxies, tunnels, digital cross connects, or even direct circuits, which separates "bad" traffic (DDoS and also other common internet attacks) and only sends good traffic beyond to the server. The provider needs central connectivity to the Internet to manage this kind of service unless they happen to be located within the same facility as the "cleaning center" or "scrubbing center".[66]

Examples of providers of this service:

- Akamai Technologies[67]
- CloudFlare[68]
- Level 3 Communications[69]
- Radware[70]
- Arbor Networks[71]
- AT&T[72]

- F5 Networks[73]
- Incapsula[74]
- Neustar Inc[75]
- Tata Communications[76]
- Verisign[77]
- Verizon[78][79]

Denial-of-service Attack, Unintentional Denial-of-service

An unintentional denial-of-service can occur when a system ends up denied, not due to a deliberate attack by a single individual or group of individuals, but simply due to a sudden enormous spike in popularity. This can happen when an extremely popular website posts a prominent link to a second, less well-prepared site, for example, as part of a news story. The result is that a significant proportion of the primary site's regular users – potentially hundreds of thousands of people – click that link in the space of a few hours, having the same effect on the target website as a DDoS attack. A VIPDoS is the same, but specifically when the link was posted by a celebrity.

When Michael Jackson died in 2009, websites such as Google and Twitter slowed down or even crashed. [80] Many sites' servers thought the requests were from a virus or spyware trying to cause a denial-of-service attack, warning users that their queries looked like "automated requests from a computer virus or spyware application".[81]

News sites and link sites – sites whose primary function is to provide links to interesting content elsewhere on the Internet – are most likely to cause this phenomenon. The canonical example is the Slashdot effect when receiving traffic from Slashdot. It is also known as "the Reddit hug of death" and "the Digg effect".

Routers have also been known to create unintentional DoS attacks, as both D-Link and Netgear routers have overloaded NTP servers by flooding NTP servers without respecting the restrictions of client types or geographical limitations.

Similar unintentional denials-of-service can also occur via other media, e.g. when a URL is mentioned on television. If a server is being indexed by Google or another search engine during peak periods of activity, or does not have a lot of available bandwidth while being indexed, it can also experience the effects of a DoS attack.[17][*citation needed*]

Legal action has been taken in at least one such case. In 2006, Universal Tube & Rollform Equipment Corporation sued YouTube: massive numbers of would-be youtube.com users accidentally typed the tube company's URL, utube.com. As a result, the tube company ended up having to spend large amounts of money on upgrading their bandwidth.[82] The company appears to have taken advantage of the situation, with utube.com now containing ads for advertisement revenue.

In March 2014, after Malaysia Airlines Flight 370 went missing, DigitalGlobe launched a crowdsourcing service on which users could help search for the missing jet in satellite images. The response overwhelmed the company's servers.[83]

An unintentional denial-of-service may also result from a prescheduled event created by the website itself, as was the case of the Census in Australia in 2016. This could be caused when a server provides some service at a specific time. This might be a university website setting the grades to be available where it will result in many more login requests at that time than any other.

Denial-of-service Attack, Side Effects of Attacks, Backscatter

In computer network security, backscatter is a side-effect of a spoofed denial-of-service attack. In this kind of attack, the attacker spoofs (or forges) the source address in IP packets sent to the victim. In general, the victim machine cannot distinguish between the spoofed packets and legitimate packets, so the victim responds to the spoofed packets as it normally would. These response packets are known as backscatter. [84]

If the attacker is spoofing source addresses randomly, the backscatter response packets from the victim will be sent back to random destinations. This effect can be used by network telescopes as indirect evidence of such attacks.

The term "backscatter analysis" refers to observing backscatter packets arriving at a statistically significant portion of the IP address space to determine characteristics of DoS attacks and victims.

Information Security, Bibliography

- Allen, Julia H. (2001). The CERT Guide to System and Network Security Practices. Boston, MA: Addison-Wesley. ISBN 0-201-73723-X.
- Krutz, Ronald L.; Russell Dean Vines (2003). The CISSP Prep Guide (Gold ed.). Indianapolis, IN: Wiley. ISBN 0-471-26802-X.
- Layton, Timothy P. (2007). Information Security: Design, Implementation, Measurement, and Compliance. Boca Raton, FL: Auerbach publications. ISBN 978-0-8493-7087-8.
- McNab, Chris (2004). Network Security Assessment. Sebastopol, CA: O'Reilly. ISBN 0-596-00611-X.
- Peltier, Thomas R. (2001). Information Security Risk Analysis. Boca Raton, FL: Auerbach publications. ISBN 0-8493-0880-1.
- Peltier, Thomas R. (2002). Information Security Policies, Procedures, and Standards: guidelines for effective information security management. Boca Raton, FL: Auerbach publications. ISBN 0-8493-1137-3.
- White, Gregory (2003). All-in-one Security+ Certification Exam Guide. Emeryville, CA: McGraw-Hill/Osborne. ISBN 0-07-222633-1.
- Dhillon, Gurpreet (2007). Principles of Information Systems Security: text and cases. NY: John Wiley & Sons. ISBN 978-0-471-45056-6.

Information Security, References

1. 44 U.S.C. § 3542(b)(1)
2. Stewart, James (2012). CISSP Study Guide. Canada: John Wiley & Sons, Inc. pp. 255–257. ISBN 978-1-118-31417-3 – via Online PSU course resource, EBL Reader.
3. Gordon, Lawrence; Loeb, Martin (November 2002). "The Economics of Information Security Investment". ACM Transactions on Information and System Security. **5** (4): 438–457. doi:10.1145/581271.581274.
4. Stewart, James (2012). CISSP Certified Information Systems Security Professional Study Guide Sixth Edition. Canada: John Wiley & Sons, Inc. pp. 255–257. ISBN 978-1-118-31417-3.
5. Suetonius Tranquillus, Gaius (2008). Lives of the Caesars (Oxford World's Classics). New York: Oxford University Press. p. 28. ISBN 978-0199537563.
6. Singh, Simon (2000). The Code Book. Anchor. pp. 289–290. ISBN 0-385-49532-3.
7. Cherdantseva Y. and Hilton J.: "Information Security and Information Assurance. The Discussion about the Meaning, Scope and Goals". In: *Organizational, Legal, and Technological Dimensions of Information System Administrator.* Almeida F., Portela, I. (eds.). IGI Global Publishing. (2013)
8. ISO/IEC 27000:2009 (E). (2009). Information technology - Security techniques - Information security management systems - Overview and vocabulary. ISO/IEC.
9. Committee on National Security Systems: National Information Assurance (IA) Glossary, CNSS Instruction No. 4009, 26 April 2010.
10. ISACA. (2008). Glossary of terms, 2008. Retrieved from http://www.isaca.org/Knowledge-Center/Documents/Glossary/glossary.pdf
11. Pipkin, D. (2000). *Information security: Protecting the global enterprise*. New York: Hewlett-Packard Company.
12. B., McDermott, E., & Geer, D. (2001). Information security is information risk management. In Proceedings of the 2001 Workshop on New Security Paradigms NSPW '01, (pp. 97 – 104). ACM. doi:10.1145/508171.508187
13. Anderson, J. M. (2003). "Why we need a new definition of information security". Computers & Security. **22** (4): 308–313. doi:10.1016/S0167-4048(03)00407-3.
14. Venter, H. S.; Eloff, J. H. P. (2003). "A taxonomy for information security technologies". Computers & Security. **22** (4): 299–307. doi:10.1016/S0167-4048(03)00406-1.
15. https://www.isc2.org/uploadedFiles/(ISC)2_Public_Content/2013%20Global%20Information%20Security%20Workforce%20Study%20Feb%202013.pdf
16. Perrin, Chad. "The CIA Triad". Retrieved 31 May 2012.
17. "Engineering Principles for Information Technology Security" (PDF). csrc.nist.gov.
18. "oecd.org" (PDF). Archived from the original (PDF) on May 16, 2011. Retrieved 2014-01-17.
19. "NIST Special Publication 800-27 Rev A" (PDF). csrc.nist.gov.
20. Aceituno, Vicente. "Open Information Security Maturity Model". Retrieved 12 February 2017.
21. Boritz, J. Efrim. "IS Practitioners' Views on Core Concepts of Information Integrity". International Journal of Accounting Information Systems. Elsevier. **6** (4): 260–279. doi:10.1016/j.accinf.2005.07.001. Retrieved 12 August 2011.
22. Loukas, G.; Oke, G. (September 2010) [August 2009]. "Protection Against Denial of Service Attacks: A Survey" (PDF). Comput. J. **53** (7): 1020–1037. doi:10.1093/comjnl/bxp078.
23. ISACA (2006). CISA Review Manual 2006. Information Systems Audit and Control Association. p. 85. ISBN 1-933284-15-3.
24. Spagnoletti, Paolo; Resca A. (2008). "The duality of Information Security Management: fighting against predictable and unpredictable threats". Journal of Information System Security. **4** (3): 46–62.
25. Kiountouzis, E.A.; Kokolakis, S.A. Information systems security: facing the information society of the 21st century. London: Chapman & Hall, Ltd. ISBN 0-412-78120-4.
26. "NIST SP 800-30 Risk Management Guide for Information Technology Systems" (PDF). Retrieved 2014-01-17.
27. [1]
28. "Segregation of Duties Control matrix". ISACA. 2008. Archived from the original on 3 July 2011. Retrieved 2008-09-30.
29. Shon Harris (2003). All-in-one CISSP Certification Exam Guide (2nd ed.). Emeryville, California: McGraw-Hill/Osborne. ISBN 0-07-222966-7.
30. itpi.org Archived December 10, 2013, at the Wayback Machine.
31. "book summary of The Visible Ops Handbook: Implementing ITIL in 4 Practical and Auditable Steps". wikisummaries.org. Retrieved 2016-06-22.
32. "The Disaster Recovery Plan". Sans Institute. Retrieved 7 February 2012.
33. Lim, Joo S., et al. "Exploring the Relationship between Organizational Culture and Information Security Culture." Australian Information Security Management Conference.
34. Cite error: The named reference Andersson_.26_Reimers_2014 was invoked but never defined (see the help page).
35. Schlienger, Thomas; Teufel, Stephanie (2003). "Information security culture-from analysis to change". South African Computer Journal. **31**: 46–52.
36. "IISP Skills Framework".
    "BSI-Standards". BSI. Retrieved 29 November 2013.

Internet Security, References

1. Gralla, Preston (2007). How the Internet Works. Indianapolis: Que Pub. ISBN 0-7897-2132-5.
2. Rhee, M. Y. (2003). Internet Security: Cryptographic Principles,Algorithms and Protocols. Chichester: Wiley. ISBN 0-470-85285-2.
3. An example of a completely re-engineered computer is the Librem laptop which uses components certified by web-security experts. It was launched after a crowd funding campaign in 2015.
4. "Information Security: A Growing Need of Businesses and Industries Worldwide". University of Alabama at Birmingham Business Program. Retrieved 20 November 2014.
5. Ramzan, Zulfikar (2010). "Phishing attacks and countermeasures". In Stamp, Mark & Stavroulakis, Peter. Handbook of Information and Communication Security. Springer. ISBN 9783642041174.
6. Van der Merwe, A J, Loock, M, Dabrowski, M. (2005), Characteristics and Responsibilities involved in a Phishing Attack, Winter International Symposium on Information and Communication Technologies, Cape Town, January 2005.
7. "2012 Global Losses From Phishing Estimated At $1.5 Bn". FirstPost. February 20, 2013. Retrieved December 21, 2014.
8. "Improving Web Application Security: Threats and Countermeasures". msdn.microsoft.com. Retrieved 2016-04-05.
9. "Justice Department charges Russian spies and criminal hackers in Yahoo intrusion". Washington Post. Retrieved 15 March 2017.
10. Margaret Rouse (September 2005). "What is a security token?". SearchSecurity.com. Retrieved 2014-02-14.
11. "Virtual Private Network". NASA. Retrieved 2014-02-14.
12. Asgaut Eng (1996-04-10). "Network Virtual Terminal". The Norwegian Institute of Technology ppv.org. Retrieved 2014-02-14.
13. "What Is a Message Authentication Code?". Wisegeek.com. Retrieved 2013-04-20.
14. "Firewalls - Internet Security". sites.google.com. Retrieved 2016-06-30.
15. "Browser Statistics". W3Schools.com. Retrieved 2011-08-10.
16. Bradly, Tony. "It's Time to Finally Drop Internet Explorer 6". PCWorld.com. Retrieved 2010-11-09.
17. Messmer, Ellen and NetworkWorld (2010-11-16). "Google Chrome Tops 'Dirty Dozen' Vulnerable Apps List". PCWorld.com. Retrieved 2010-11-09.
18. Keizer, Greg (2009-07-15). "Firefox 3.5 Vulnerability Confirmed". PCWorld.com. Retrieved 2010-11-09.
19. Skinner, Carrie-Ann. "Opera Plugs "Severe" Browser Hole". PC World.com. Archived from the original on May 20, 2009. Retrieved 2010-11-09.
20. Larkin, Eric (2008-08-26). "Build Your Own Free Security Suite". Retrieved 2010-11-09.
21. "USE A FREE PASSWORD MANAGER" (PDF). scscbkk.org.
22. Rebbapragada, Narasu. "All-in-one Security". PC World.com. Archived from the original on October 27, 2010. Retrieved 2010-11-09.
23. "Free products for PC security". 2015-10-08.

Computer Security, References

1. Gasser, Morrie (1988). Building a Secure Computer System (PDF). Van Nostrand Reinhold. p. 3. ISBN 0-442-23022-2. Retrieved 6 September 2015.
2. "Definition of computer security". Encyclopedia. Ziff Davis, PCMag. Retrieved 6 September 2015.
3. Rouse, Margaret. "Social engineering definition". TechTarget. Retrieved 6 September 2015.
4. "Reliance spells end of road for ICT amateurs", May 07, 2013, The Australian
5. "Computer Security and Mobile Security Challenges" (pdf). researchgate.net. Retrieved 2016-08-04.
6. "Distributed Denial of Service Attack". csa.gov.sg. Retrieved 12 November 2014.
7. Wireless mouse leave billions at risk of computer hack: cyber security firm
8. "What is Spoofing? – Definition from Techopedia".
9. Gallagher, Sean (May 14, 2014). "Photos of an NSA "upgrade" factory show Cisco router getting implant". Ars Technica. Retrieved August 3, 2014.
10. "Identifying Phishing Attempts". Case.
11. Arcos Sergio. "Social Engineering" (PDF).
12. Scannell, Kara (24 Feb 2016). "CEO email scam costs companies $2bn". Financial Times (25 Feb 2016). Retrieved 7 May 2016.
13. "Bucks leak tax info of players, employees as result of email scam". Associated Press. 20 May 2016. Retrieved 20 May 2016.
14. Lim, Joo S., et al. "Exploring the Relationship between Organizational Culture and Information Security Culture." Australian Information Security Management Conference.
15. Cite error: The named reference Andersson_.26_Reimers_2014 was invoked but never defined (see the help page).
16. Schlienger, Thomas; Teufel, Stephanie (2003). "Information security culture-from analysis to change". South African Computer Journal. **31**: 46–52.
17. "Financial Weapons of War". Minnesota Law Review. 2016. SSRN 2765010.
18. Pagliery, Jose. "Hackers attacked the U.S. energy grid 79 times this year". CNN Money. Cable News Network. Retrieved 16 April 2015.
19. "Vulnerabilities in Smart Meters and the C12.12 Protocol". SecureState. 2012-02-16. Retrieved 4 November 2016.
20. P. G. Neumann, "Computer Security in Aviation," presented at International Conference on Aviation Safety and Security in the 21st Century, White House Commission on Safety and Security, 1997.
21. J. Zellan, Aviation Security. Hauppauge, NY: Nova Science, 2003, pp. 65–70.
22. "Air Traffic Control Systems Vulnerabilities Could Make for Unfriendly Skies [Black Hat] - SecurityWeek.Com".
23. "Hacker Says He Can Break Into Airplane Systems Using In-Flight Wi-Fi". NPR.org. 4 August 2014.
24. Jim Finkle (4 August 2014). "Hacker says to show passenger jets at risk of cyber attack". Reuters.
25. "Pan-European Network Services (PENS) - Eurocontrol.int".
26. "Centralised Services: NewPENS moves forward - Eurocontrol.int".
27. "NextGen Data Communication". FAA.
28. "Is Your Watch Or Thermostat A Spy? Cybersecurity Firms Are On It". NPR.org. 6 August 2014.
29. Melvin Backman (18 September 2014). "Home Depot: 56 million cards exposed in breach". CNNMoney.
30. "Staples: Breach may have affected 1.16 million customers' cards". Fortune.com. December 19, 2014. Retrieved 2014-12-21.
31. "Target security breach affects up to 40M cards". Associated Press via Milwaukee Journal Sentinel. 19 December 2013. Retrieved 21 December 2013.
32. Jim Finkle (23 April 2014). "Exclusive: FBI warns healthcare sector vulnerable to cyber attacks". Reuters. Retrieved 23 May 2016.
33. Bright, Peter (February 15, 2011). "Anonymous speaks: the inside story of the HBGary hack". Arstechnica.com. Retrieved March 29, 2011.
34. Anderson, Nate (February 9, 2011). "How one man tracked down Anonymous—and paid a heavy price". Arstechnica.com. Retrieved March 29, 2011.
35. Palilery, Jose (December 24, 2014). "What caused Sony hack: What we know now". CNN Money. Retrieved January 4, 2015.
36. James Cook (December 16, 2014). "Sony Hackers Have Over 100 Terabytes Of Documents. Only Released 200 Gigabytes So Far". Business Insider. Retrieved December 18, 2014.
37. Timothy B. Lee (18 January 2015). "The next frontier of hacking: your car". Vox.
38. Tracking & Hacking: Security & Privacy Gaps Put American Drivers at Risk (PDF) (Report). 2015-02-06. Retrieved November 4, 2016.
39. Staff, AOL. "Cybersecurity expert: It will take a 'major event' for companies to take this issue seriously". AOL.com. Retrieved 22 January 2017.
40. "The problem with self-driving cars: who controls the code?". The Guardian. 23 December 2015. Retrieved 22 January 2017.
41. Stephen Checkoway; Damon McCoy; Brian Kantor; Danny Anderson; Hovav Shacham; Stefan Savage; Karl Koscher; Alexei Czeskis; Franziska Roesner; Tadayoshi Kohno (2011). Comprehensive Experimental Analyses of Automotive Attack Surfaces (PDF). SEC'11 Proceedings of the 20th USENIX conference on Security. Berkeley, CA, US: USENIX Association. pp. 6–6.
42. Greenberg, Andy. "Hackers Remotely Kill a Jeep on the Highway—With Me in It". WIRED. Retrieved 22 January 2017.
43. "Hackers take control of car, drive it into a ditch". The Independent. 22 July 2015. Retrieved 22 January 2017.
44. "Tesla fixes software bug that allowed Chinese hackers to control car remotely". The Telegraph. Retrieved 22 January 2017.
45. Kang, Cecilia (19 September 2016). "Self-Driving Cars Gain Powerful Ally: The Government". The New York Times. Retrieved 22 January 2017.
46. "Federal Automated Vehicles Policy" (PDF). Retrieved 22 January 2017.
47. "Internet strikes back: Anonymous' Operation Megaupload explained". RT. 20 January 2012. Archived from the original on 5 May 2013. Retrieved May 5, 2013.
48. "Gary McKinnon profile: Autistic 'hacker' who started writing computer programs at 14". The Daily Telegraph. London. 23 January 2009.
49. "Gary McKinnon extradition ruling due by 16 October". BBC News. September 6, 2012. Retrieved September 25, 2012.
50. Law Lords Department (30 July 2008). "House of Lords – Mckinnon V Government of The United States of America and Another". Publications.parliament.uk. Retrieved 30 January 2010. 15. … alleged to total over $700,000
51. "NSA Accessed Mexican President's Email", October 20, 2013, Jens Glüsing, Laura Poitras, Marcel Rosenbach and Holger Stark, spiegel.de
52. Sanders, Sam (4 June 2015). "Massive Data Breach Puts 4 Million Federal Employees' Records At Risk". NPR. Retrieved 5 June 2015.
53. Liptak, Kevin (4 June 2015). "U.S. government hacked; feds think China is the culprit". CNN. Retrieved 5 June 2015.
54. Sean Gallagher. "Encryption "would not have helped" at OPM, says DHS official".
55. "Schools Learn Lessons From Security Breaches". Education Week. 19 October 2015. Retrieved 23 May 2016.
56. "Internet of Things Global Standards Initiative". ITU. Retrieved 26 June 2015.
57. Singh, Jatinder; Pasquier, Thomas; Bacon, Jean; Ko, Hajoon; Eyers, David (2015). "Twenty Cloud Security Considerations for Supporting the Internet of Things". IEEE Internet of Things Journal: 1–1. doi:10.1109/JIOT.2015.2460333.
58. Chris Clearfield. "Why The FTC Can't Regulate The Internet Of Things". Forbes. Retrieved 26 June 2015.
59. "Internet of Things: Science Fiction or Business Fact?" (PDF). Harvard Business Review. Retrieved 4 November 2016.
60. Ovidiu Vermesan; Peter Friess. "Internet of Things: Converging Technologies for Smart Environments and Integrated Ecosystems" (PDF). River Publishers. Retrieved 4 November 2016.
61. Christopher Clearfield "Rethinking Security for the Internet of Things" Harvard Business Review Blog, 26 June 2013/
62. "Hotel room burglars exploit critical flaw in electronic door locks". Ars Technica. Retrieved 23 May 2016.
63. "Hospital Medical Devices Used As Weapons In Cyberattacks". Dark Reading. Retrieved 23 May 2016.
64. Jeremy Kirk (17 October 2012). "Pacemaker hack can deliver deadly 830-volt jolt". Computerworld. Retrieved 23 May 2016.
65. "How Your Pacemaker Will Get Hacked". The Daily Beast. Retrieved 23 May 2016.
66. Leetaru, Kalev. "Hacking Hospitals And Holding Hostages: Cybersecurity In 2016". Forbes. Retrieved 29 December 2016.
67. "Cyber-Angriffe: Krankenhäuser rücken ins Visier der Hacker". Wirtschafts Woche. Retrieved 29 December 2016.
68. "Hospitals keep getting attacked by ransomware — Here's why". Business Insider. Retrieved 29 December 2016.
69. "MedStar Hospitals Recovering After 'Ransomware' Hack". NBC News. Retrieved 29 December 2016.
70. Pauli, Darren. "US hospitals hacked with ancient exploits". The Register. Retrieved 29 December 2016.
71. Pauli, Darren. "Zombie OS lurches through Royal Melbourne Hospital spreading virus". The Register. Retrieved 29 December 2016.
72. "Grimsby hospital computer attack: 'No ransom has been demanded'". Grimsby Telegraph. 31 October 2016. Retrieved 29 December 2016.
73. "Hacked Lincolnshire hospital computer systems 'back up'". BBC News. 2 November 2016. Retrieved 29 December 2016.
74. "Lincolnshire operations cancelled after network attack". BBC News. 31 October 2016. Retrieved 29 December 2016.
75. "Legion cyber-attack: Next dump is sansad.nic.in, say hackers". The Indian Express. 12 December 2016. Retrieved 29 December 2016.
76. "15k patients' info shared on social media from NH Hospital data breach". RT International. Retrieved 29 December 2016.
77. "Former New Hampshire Psychiatric Hospital Patient Accused Of Data Breach". CBS Boston. Retrieved 29 December 2016.
78. "Texas Hospital hacked, affects nearly 30,000 patient records". Healthcare IT News. 4 November 2016. Retrieved 29 December 2016.

79. Becker, Rachel (27 December 2016). "New cybersecurity guidelines for medical devices tackle evolving threats". The Verge. Retrieved 29 December 2016.
80. "Postmarket Management of Cybersecurity in Medical Devices" (PDF). 28 December 2016. Retrieved 29 December 2016.
81. Cashell, B., Jackson, W. D., Jickling, M., & Webel, B. (2004). The Economic Impact of Cyber-Attacks. Congressional Research Service, Government and Finance Division. Washington DC: The Library of Congress.
82. Gordon, Lawrence; Loeb, Martin (November 2002). "The Economics of Information Security Investment". ACM Transactions on Information and System Security. **5** (4): 438–457. doi:10.1145/581271.581274.
83. RFC 2828 Internet Security Glossary
84. CNSS Instruction No. 4009 dated 26 April 2010
85. InfosecToday Glossary
86. Definitions: IT Security Architecture. SecurityArchitecture.org, Jan, 2006
87. Jannsen, Cory. "Security Architecture". Techopedia. Janalta Interactive Inc. Retrieved 9 October 2014.
88. "Cybersecurity at petabyte scale".
89. Woodie, Alex (9 May 2016). "Why ONI May Be Our Best Hope for Cyber Security Now". Retrieved 13 July 2016.
90. "Firms lose more to electronic than physical theft". Reuters.
91. Foreman, P: *Vulnerability Management*, page 1. Taylor & Francis Group, 2010. ISBN 978-1-4398-0150-5
92. Anna-Maija Juuso and Ari Takanen *Unknown Vulnerability Management*, Codenomicon whitepaper, October 2010 [1].
93. Alan Calder and Geraint Williams. PCI DSS: A Pocket Guide, 3rd Edition. ISBN 978-1-84928-554-4. network vulnerability scans at least quarterly and after any significant change in the network
94. Harrison, J. (2003). "Formal verification at Intel": 45–54. doi:10.1109/LICS.2003.1210044.
95. Umrigar, Zerksis D.; Pitchumani, Vijay (1983). "Formal verification of a real-time hardware design". Proceeding DAC '83 Proceedings of the 20th Design Automation Conference. IEEE Press. pp. 221–7. ISBN 0-8186-0026-8.
96. "Abstract Formal Specification of the seL4/ARMv6 API" (PDF). Archived from the original (PDF) on 21 May 2015. Retrieved May 19, 2015.
97. Christoph Baumann, Bernhard Beckert, Holger Blasum, and Thorsten Bormer Ingredients of Operating System Correctness? Lessons Learned in the Formal Verification of PikeOS
98. "Getting it Right" by Jack Ganssle
99. Treglia, J., & Delia, M. (2017). Cyber Security Inoculation. Presented at NYS Cyber Security Conference, Empire State Plaza Convention Center, Albany, NY, June 3–4.
100. "The Hacker in Your Hardware: The Next Security Threat". Scientific American.
101. Waksman, Adam; Sethumadhavan, Simha (2010), "Tamper Evident Microprocessors" (PDF), Proceedings of the IEEE Symposium on Security and Privacy, Oakland, California
102. "Sentinel HASP HL". E-Spin. Retrieved 2014-03-20.
103. "Token-based authentication". SafeNet.com. Retrieved 2014-03-20.
104. "Lock and protect your Windows PC". TheWindowsClub.com. Retrieved 2014-03-20.
105. James Greene (2012). "Intel Trusted Execution Technology: White Paper" (PDF). Intel Corporation. Retrieved 2013-12-18.
106. "SafeNet ProtectDrive 8.4". SCMagazine.com. 2008-10-04. Retrieved 2014-03-20.
107. "Secure Hard Drives: Lock Down Your Data". PCMag.com. 2009-05-11.
108. "Top 10 vulnerabilities inside the network". Network World. 2010-11-08. Retrieved 2014-03-20.
109. "Forget IDs, use your phone as credentials". Fox Business Network. 2013-11-04. Retrieved 2014-03-20.
110. Lipner, Steve (2015). "The Birth and Death of the Orange Book". IEEE Annals of the History of Computing. **37** (2): 19–31. doi:10.1109/MAHC.2015.27.
111. Kelly Jackson Higgins (2008-11-18). "Secure OS Gets Highest NSA Rating, Goes Commercial". Dark Reading. Retrieved 2013-12-01.
112. "Board or bored? Lockheed Martin gets into the COTS hardware biz". VITA Technologies Magazine. December 10, 2010. Retrieved 9 March 2012.
113. Sanghavi, Alok (21 May 2010). "What is formal verification?". EE Times_Asia.
114. Jonathan Zittrain, 'The Future of The Internet', Penguin Books, 2008
115. Information Security. United States Department of Defense, 1986
116. "THE TJX COMPANIES, INC. VICTIMIZED BY COMPUTER SYSTEMS INTRUSION; PROVIDES INFORMATION TO HELP PROTECT CUSTOMERS" (Press release). The TJX Companies, Inc. 2007-01-17. Retrieved 2009-12-12.
117. Largest Customer Info Breach Grows. MyFox Twin Cities, 29 March 2007.
118. "The Stuxnet Attack On Iran's Nuclear Plant Was 'Far More Dangerous' Than Previously Thought". Business Insider. 20 November 2013.
119. Reals, Tucker (24 September 2010). "Stuxnet Worm a U.S. Cyber-Attack on Iran Nukes?". CBS News.
120. Kim Zetter (17 February 2011). "Cyberwar Issues Likely to Be Addressed Only After a Catastrophe". Wired. Retrieved 18 February 2011.
121. Chris Carroll (18 October 2011). "Cone of silence surrounds U.S. cyberwarfare". Stars and Stripes. Retrieved 30 October 2011.
122. John Bumgarner (27 April 2010). "Computers as Weapons of War" (PDF). IO Journal. Retrieved 30 October 2011.
123. Greenwald, Glenn. "NSA collecting phone records of millions of Verizon customers daily". The Guardian. Retrieved August 16, 2013. Exclusive: Top secret court order requiring Verizon to hand over all call data shows scale of domestic surveillance under Obama
124. Seipel, Hubert. "Transcript: ARD interview with Edward Snowden". La Foundation Courage. Retrieved 11 June 2014.
125. Newman, Lily Hay (9 October 2013). "Can You Trust NIST?". IEEE Spectrum.
126. "New Snowden Leak: NSA Tapped Google, Yahoo Data Centers", Oct 31, 2013, Lorenzo Franceschi-Bicchierai, mashable.com
127. Michael Riley; Ben Elgin; Dune Lawrence; Carol Matlack. "Target Missed Warnings in Epic Hack of Credit Card Data – Businessweek". Businessweek.com.
128. "Home Depot says 53 million emails stolen". CNET. CBS Interactive. 6 November 2014.
129. "Millions more Americans hit by government personnel data hack". Reuters. 2017-07-09. Retrieved 2017-02-25.
130. Barrett, Devlin. "U.S. Suspects Hackers in China Breached About four (4) Million People's Records, Officials Say". The Wall Street Journal.
131. Risen, Tom (5 June 2015). "China Suspected in Theft of Federal Employee Records". US News & World Report. Archived from the original on 2015-06-06.
132. Zengerle, Patricia (2015-07-19). "Estimate of Americans hit by government personnel data hack skyrockets". Reuters.
133. Sanger, David (5 June 2015). "Hacking Linked to China Exposes Millions of U.S. Workers". New York Times.
134. Mansfield-Devine, Steve (2015-09-01). "The Ashley Madison affair". Network Security. **2015** (9): 8–16. doi:10.1016/S1353-4858(15)30080-5.
135. "Mikko Hypponen: Fighting viruses, defending the net". TED.
136. "Mikko Hypponen – Behind Enemy Lines". Hack In The Box Security Conference.
137. "Ensuring the Security of Federal Information Systems and Cyber Critical Infrastructure and Protecting the Privacy of Personally Identifiable Information". Government Accountability Office. Retrieved November 3, 2015.
138. Kirby, Carrie (June 24, 2011). "Former White House aide backs some Net regulation / Clarke says government, industry deserve 'F' in cyber security". The San Francisco Chronicle.
139. "FIRST website".
140. "First members".
141. "European council".
142. "MAAWG".
143. "MAAWG".
144. "Government of Canada Launches Canada's Cyber Security Strategy". Market Wired. 3 October 2010. Retrieved 1 November 2014.
145. "Canada's Cyber Security Strategy". Public Safety Canada. Government of Canada. Retrieved 1 November 2014.
146. "Action Plan 2010–2015 for Canada's Cyber Security Strategy". Public Safety Canada. Government of Canada. Retrieved 3 November 2014.
147. "Cyber Incident Management Framework For Canada". Public Safety Canada. Government of Canada. Retrieved 3 November 2014.
148. "Action Plan 2010–2015 for Canada's Cyber Security Strategy". Public Safety Canada. Government of Canada. Retrieved 1 November 2014.
149. "Canadian Cyber Incident Response Centre". Public Safety Canada. Retrieved 1 November 2014.
150. "Cyber Security Bulletins". Public Safety Canada. Retrieved 1 November 2014.
151. "Report a Cyber Security Incident". Public Safety Canada. Government of Canada. Retrieved 3 November 2014.
152. "Government of Canada Launches Cyber Security Awareness Month With New Public Awareness Partnership". Market Wired. Government of Canada. 27 September 2012. Retrieved 3 November 2014.
153. "Cyber Security Cooperation Program". Public Safety Canada. Retrieved 1 November 2014.
154. "Cyber Security Cooperation Program". Public Safety Canada.
155. "GetCyberSafe". Get Cyber Safe. Government of Canada. Retrieved 3 November 2014.
156. "6.16 Internet security: National IT independence and China's cyber policy," in: Sebastian Heilmann, editor, China*'s Political System,* Lanham, Boulder, New York, London: Rowman & Littlefield Publishers (2017) ISBN 978-1442277342
157. "Cyber Security". Tier3 — Cyber Security Services Pakistan.
158. "National Response Centre For Cyber Crime".
159. "Tier3 – Cyber Security Services Pakistan". Tier3 – Cyber Security Services Pakistan.
160. "Surfsafe® Pakistan". Surfsafe® Pakistan-report terrorist and extremist online-content.
161. "South Korea seeks global support in cyber attack probe". BBC Monitoring Asia Pacific. 7 March 2011.
162. Kwanwoo Jun (23 September 2013). "Seoul Puts a Price on Cyberdefense". Wall Street Journal. Dow Jones & Company, Inc. Retrieved 24 September 2013.
163. "Text of H.R.4962 as Introduced in House: International Cybercrime Reporting and Cooperation Act – U.S. Congress". OpenCongress. Archived from the original on 2010-12-28. Retrieved 2013-09-25.
164. [2] Archived 20 January 2012 at the Wayback Machine.
165. "National Cyber Security Division". U.S. Department of Homeland Security. Archived from the original on 11 June 2008. Retrieved June 14, 2008.
166. "FAQ: Cyber Security R&D Center". U.S. Department of Homeland Security S&T Directorate. Retrieved June 14, 2008.
167. AFP-JiJi, "U.S. boots up cybersecurity center", October 31, 2009.
168. "Federal Bureau of Investigation – Priorities". Federal Bureau of Investigation.
169. "Internet Crime Complaint Center (IC3) – Home".
170. "Infragard, Official Site". Infragard. Retrieved 10 September 2010.
171. "Robert S. Mueller, III – InfraGard Interview at the 2005 InfraGard Conference". Infragard (Official Site) – "Media Room". Archived from the original on 17 June 2011. Retrieved 9 December 2009.
172. "CCIPS".
173. "U.S. Department of Defense, Cyber Command Fact Sheet". stratcom.mil. 21 May 2010. Archived from the original on 19 December 2013.
174. "Speech:". Defense.gov. Retrieved 2010-07-10.
175. Shachtman, Noah. "Military's Cyber Commander Swears: "No Role" in Civilian Networks", The Brookings Institution, 23 September 2010.
176. "FCC Cybersecurity". FCC.
177. "Cybersecurity for Medical Devices and Hospital Networks: FDA Safety Communication". Retrieved 23 May 2016.
178. "Automotive Cybersecurity – National Highway Traffic Safety Administration (NHTSA)". Retrieved 23 May 2016.
179. "U.S. GAO – Air Traffic Control: FAA Needs a More Comprehensive Approach to Address Cybersecurity As Agency Transitions to NextGen". Retrieved 23 May 2016.
180. Aliya Sternstein (4 March 2016). "FAA Working on New Guidelines for Hack-Proof Planes". Nextgov. Retrieved 23 May 2016.
181. Bart Elias (18 June 2015). "Protecting Civil Aviation from Cyberattacks" (PDF). Retrieved 4 November 2016.
182. Verton, Dan (January 28, 2004). "DHS launches national cyber alert system". Computerworld. IDG. Retrieved 2008-06-15.
183. Clayton, Mark. "The new cyber arms race". The Christian Science Monitor. Retrieved 16 April 2015.
184. Nakashima, Ellen (September 13, 2016). "Obama to be urged to split cyberwar command from NSA". The Washington Post. Archived from the original on September 14, 2016.
185. "Burning Glass Technologies, "Cybersecurity Jobs, 2015"". July 2015. Retrieved 11 June 2016.
186. Oltsik, Jon. "Cybersecurity Skills Shortage Impact on Cloud Computing". Network World. Retrieved 2016-03-23.
187. [3] Burning Glass Technologies, "Demand for Cybersecurity Workers Outstripping Supply," July 30, 2015, accessed 2016-06-11
188. de Silva, Richard (11 Oct 2011). "Government vs. Commerce: The Cyber Security Industry and You (Part One)". Defence IQ. Retrieved 24 Apr 2014.
189. http://iase.disa.mil/iawip/Pages/iabaseline.aspx
190. "Department of Computer Science". Retrieved April 30, 2013.
191. "(Information for) Students". NICCS (US National Initiative for Cybercareers and Studies). Retrieved 24 April 2014.
192. "Current Job Opportunities at DHS". U.S. Department of Homeland Security. Retrieved 2013-05-05.
193. "Cybersecurity Training & Exercises". U.S. Department of Homeland Security. Retrieved 2015-01-09.
194. "Cyber Security Awareness Free Training and Webcasts". MS-ISAC (Multi-State Information Sharing & Analysis Center). Retrieved 9 January 2015.
195. "Security Training Courses". LearnQuest. Retrieved 2015-01-09.
196. "Confidentiality". Retrieved 2011-10-31.
197. "Data Integrity". Retrieved 2011-10-31.
"Endpoint Security". Retrieved 2014-03-15.

Mobile Security, Notes

1. Steven., Furnell, (2009-01-01). Mobile security. IT Governance Pub. ISBN 9781849280204. OCLC 704518497.
2. BYOD and Increased Malware Threats Help Driving Billion Dollar Mobile Security Services Market in 2013, ABI Research
3. Bishop 2004.
4. Olson, Parmy. "Your smartphone is hackers' next big target". CNN. Retrieved August 26, 2013.
5. (PDF) http://www.gov.mu/portal/sites/cert/files/Guide%20on%20Protection%20Against%20Hacking.pdf. Missing or empty |title= (help)
6. Lemos, Robert. "New laws make hacking a black-and-white choice". CNET News.com. Retrieved September 23, 2002.
7. McCaney, Kevin. "'Unknowns' hack NASA, Air Force, saying 'We're here to help'". Retrieved May 7, 2012.
8. Bilton 2010.
9. Guo, Wang & Zhu 2004, p. 3.
10. Dagon, Martin & Starder 2004, p. 12.
11. Dixon & Mishra 2010, p. 3.
12. Töyssy & Helenius 2006, p. 113.
13. Siemens 2010, p. 1.
14. "Brookstone spy tank app". limormoyal.com. Retrieved 2016-08-11.
15. Gendrullis 2008, p. 266.
16. European Telecommunications Standards Institute 2011, p. 1.
17. Jøsang, Miralabé & Dallot 2015.
18. Roth, Polak & Rieffel 2008, p. 220.
19. Gittleson, Kim (28 March 2014) Data-stealing Snoopy drone unveiled at Black Hat BBC News, Technology, Retrieved 29 March 2014
20. Wilkinson, Glenn (25 September 2012) Snoopy: A distributed tracking and profiling framework Sensepost, Retrieved 29 March 2014
21. Töyssy & Helenius 2006, p. 27.
22. Mulliner 2006, p. 113.
23. Dunham, Abu Nimeh & Becher 2008, p. 225.
24. Becher 2009, p. 65.
25. Becher 2009, p. 66.
26. Kasmi C, Lopes Esteves J (13 August 2015). "IEMI Threats for Information Security: Remote Command Injection on Modern Smartphones". IEEE Transactions on Electromagnetic Compatibility. doi:10.1109/TEMC.2015.2463089. Lay summary – WIRED (14 October 2015).
27. Aviv, Adam J.; Gibson, Katherine; Mossop, Evan; Blaze, Matt; Smith, Jonathan M. Smudge Attacks on Smartphone Touch Screens (PDF). 4th USENIX Workshop on Offensive Technologies.
28. Schmidt et al. 2009a, p. 3.
29. Suarez-Tangil, Guillermo; Juan E. Tapiador; Pedro Peris-Lopez; Arturo Ribagorda (2014). "Evolution, Detection and Analysis of Malware in Smart Devices" (PDF). IEEE Communications Surveys & Tutorials.
30. Becher 2009, p. 87.
31. Becher 2009, p. 88.
32. Mickens & Noble 2005, p. 1.
33. Raboin 2009, p. 272.
34. Töyssy & Helenius 2006, p. 114.

35. Haas, Peter D. (2015-01-01). "Ransomware goes mobile: An analysis of the threats posed by emerging methods". UTICA COLLEGE.
36. Becher 2009, p. 91-94.
37. Becher 2009, p. 12.
38. Schmidt, Schmidt & Clausen 2008, p. 5-6.
39. Halbronn & Sigwald 2010, p. 5-6.
40. Ruff 2011, p. 127.
41. Hogben & Dekker 2010, p. 50.
42. Schmidt, Schmidt & Clausen 2008, p. 50.
43. Shabtai et al. 2009, p. 10.
44. Becher 2009, p. 31.
45. Schmidt, Schmidt & Clausen 2008, p. 3.
46. Shabtai et al. 2009, p. 7-8.
47. Pandya 2008, p. 15.
48. Becher 2009, p. 22.
49. Becher et al. 2011, p. 96.
50. Becher 2009, p. 128.
51. Becher 2009, p. 140.
52. Thirumathyam & Derawi 2010, p. 1.
53. Schmidt, Schmidt & Clausen 2008, p. 7-12.
54. Becher 2009, p. 126.
55. Malik 2016, p. 28.
56. Becher et al. 2011, p. 101.
57. Ruff 2011, p. 11.
58. Hogben & Dekker 2010, p. 45.
59. Becher 2009, p. 13.
60. Becher 2009, p. 34.
61. Ruff 2011, p. 7.
62. Hogben & Dekker 2010, p. 46-48.
63. Ruff 2011, p. 7-8.
64. Shabtai et al. 2009, p. 8-9.
65. Hogben & Dekker 2010, p. 43.
66. Hogben & Dekker 2010, p. 47.
67. Hogben & Dekker 2010, p. 43-45.
68. Charlie Sorrel (2010-03-01). "TigerText Deletes Text Messages From Receiver's Phone". Wired. Archived from the original on 2010-10-17. Retrieved 2010-03-02.
69. Becher 2009, p. 40.
70. Gupta 2016, p. 461.

Computer Virus, References

1. Stallings, William (2012). Computer security : principles and practice. Boston: Pearson. p. 182. ISBN 978-0-13-277506-9.
2. Aycock, John (2006). Computer Viruses and Malware. Springer. p. 14. ISBN 978-0-387-30236-2.
3. "Archived copy". Archived from the original on 2008-08-04. Retrieved 2014-07-17.
4. "Alan Solomon 'All About Viruses' (VX heavens)". Web.archive.org. 2011-06-14. Archived from the original on January 17, 2012. Retrieved 2014-07-17.
5. Mookhey, K.K. et al. (2005). Linux: Security, Audit and Control Features. ISACA. p. 128. ISBN 9781893209787.
6. Toxen, Bob (2003). Real World Linux Security: Intrusion Prevention, Detection, and Recovery. Prentice Hall Professional. p. 365. ISBN 9780130464569.
7. Noyes, Katherine (Aug 3, 2010). "Why Linux Is More Secure Than Windows". PCWorld.
8. Skoudis, Edward (2004). "Infection mechanisms and targets". Malware: Fighting Malicious Code. Prentice Hall Professional. pp. 31–48. ISBN 9780131014053.
9. Aycock, John (2006). Computer Viruses and Malware. Springer. p. 27. ISBN 978-0-387-30236-2.
10. Ludwig, Mark A. (1996). The Little Black Book of Computer Viruses: Volume 1, The Basic Technologies. pp. 16–17. ISBN 0-929408-02-0.
11. Harley, David et al. (2001). Viruses Revealed. McGraw-Hill. p. 6. ISBN 0-07-222818-0.
12. Filiol, Eric (2005). Computer viruses:from theory to applications. Springer. p. 8. ISBN 978-2-287-23939-7.
13. Bell, David J. et al, eds. (2004). "Virus". Cyberculture: The Key Concepts. Routledge. p. 154. ISBN 9780203647059.
14. "Viruses that can cost you".
15. Granneman, Scott. "Linux vs. Windows Viruses". The Register. Retrieved September 4, 2015.
16. Kaspersky, Eugene (November 21, 2005). "The contemporary antivirus industry and its problems". SecureLight.
17. Ludwig, Mark (1998). The giant black book of computer viruses. Show Low, Ariz: American Eagle. p. 13. ISBN 978-0-929408-23-1.
18. The term "computer virus" was not used at that time.
19. von Neumann, John (1966). "Theory of Self-Reproducing Automata" (PDF). Essays on Cellular Automata. University of Illinois Press: 66–87. Retrieved June 10, 2010.
20. Éric Filiol, Computer viruses: from theory to applications, Volume 1, Birkhäuser, 2005, pp. 19–38 ISBN 2-287-23939-1.
21. Risak, Veith (1972), "Selbstreproduzierende Automaten mit minimaler Informationsübertragung", Zeitschrift für Maschinenbau und Elektrotechnik
22. Kraus, Jürgen (February 1980), Selbstreproduktion bei Programmen (PDF)
23. "Virus list". Retrieved 2008-02-07.
24. Thomas Chen, Jean-Marc Robert (2004). "The Evolution of Viruses and Worms". Retrieved 2009-02-16.
25. Parikka, Jussi (2007). Digital Contagions: A Media Archaeology of Computer Viruses. New York: Peter Lang. p. 50. ISBN 978-0-8204-8837-0.
26. Russell, Deborah & Gangemi, G.T. (1991). Computer Security Basics. O'Reilly. p. 86. ISBN 0-937175-71-4.
27. IMDB synopsis of Westworld. Retrieved November 28, 2015.
28. Michael Crichton (November 21, 1973). Westworld (movie). 201 S. Kinney Road, Tucson, Arizona, USA: Metro-Goldwyn-Mayer. Event occurs at 32 minutes. And there's a clear pattern here which suggests an analogy to an infectious disease process, spreading from one resort area to the next." ... "Perhaps there are superficial similarities to disease." "I must confess I find it difficult to belief in a disease of machinery.
29. Anick Jesdanun (1 September 2007). "School prank starts 25 years of security woes". CNBC. Retrieved April 12, 2013.
30. "The anniversary of a nuisance". [permanent dead link]
31. Cohen, Fred (1984), Computer Viruses – Theory and Experiments
32. Cohen, Fred, An Undetectable Computer Virus, 1987, IBM
33. Burger, Ralph, 1991. Computer Viruses and Data Protection, pp. 19–20
34. Dr. Solomon's Virus Encyclopedia, 1995. ISBN 1-897661-00-2. Abstract. Archived August 4, 2008, at the Wayback Machine.
35. Gunn, J.B. (June 1984). "Use of virus functions to provide a virtual APL interpreter under user control". ACM SIGAPL APL Quote Quad archive. ACM New York, NY, USA. **14** (4): 163–168. ISSN 0163-6006. doi:10.1145/384283.801093.
36. "Boot sector virus repair". Antivirus.about.com. 2010-06-10. Retrieved 2010-08-27.
37. "Amjad Farooq Alvi Inventor of first PC Virus post by Zagham". YouTube. Retrieved 2010-08-27.
38. "winvir virus". Retrieved 10 June 2016.
39. Grimes, Roger (2001). Malicious Mobile Code: Virus Protection for Windows. O'Reilly. pp. 99–100. ISBN 9781565926820.
40. "SCA virus". Virus Test Center, University of Hamburg. 1990-06-05. Retrieved 2014-01-14.
41. http://5-0-1.webs.com
42. Ludwig, Mark (1998). The giant black book of computer viruses. Show Low, Ariz: American Eagle. p. 15. ISBN 978-0-929408-23-1.
43. Stallings, William (2012). Computer security : principles and practice. Boston: Pearson. p. 183. ISBN 978-0-13-277506-9.
44. Ludwig, Mark (1998). The giant black book of computer viruses. Show Low, Ariz: American Eagle. p. 292. ISBN 978-0-929408-23-1.
45. "www.cs.colostate.edu" (PDF). Retrieved 2016-04-25.
46. Gregory, Peter (2004). Computer viruses for dummies (in Danish). Hoboken, NJ: Wiley Pub. p. 210. ISBN 0-7645-7418-3.
47. Szor, Peter (2005). The art of computer virus research and defense. Upper Saddle River, NJ: Addison-Wesley. p. 43. ISBN 0-321-30454-3.
48. Serazzi, Giuseppe & Zanero, Stefano (2004). "Computer Virus Propagation Models". In Calzarossa, Maria Carla & Gelenbe, Erol. Performance Tools and Applications to Networked Systems (PDF). Lecture Notes in Computer Science. Vol. 2965. pp. 26–50.
49. Avoine, Gildas et al. (2007). Computer System Security: Basic Concepts and Solved Exercises. EPFL Press / CRC Press. pp. 21–22. ISBN 9781420046205.
50. Brain, Marshall; Fenton, Wesley. "How Computer Viruses Work". HowStuffWorks.com. Retrieved 16 June 2013.
51. Grimes, Roger (2001). Malicious Mobile Code: Virus Protection for Windows. O'Reilly. pp. 37–38. ISBN 9781565926820.
52. Salomon, David (2006). Foundations of Computer Security. Springer. pp. 47–48. ISBN 9781846283413.
53. Polk, William T. (1995). Antivirus Tools and Techniques for Computer Systems. William Andrew (Elsevier). p. 4. ISBN 9780815513643.
54. Grimes, Roger (2001). "Macro Viruses". Malicious Mobile Code: Virus Protection for Windows. O'Reilly. ISBN 9781565926820.
55. Aycock, John (2006). Computer Viruses and Malware. Springer. p. 89. ISBN 9780387341880.
56. "What is boot sector virus?". Retrieved 2015-10-16.
57. Anonymous (2003). Maximum Security. Sams Publishing. pp. 331–333. ISBN 9780672324598.
58. Skoudis, Edward (2004). "Infection mechanisms and targets". Malware: Fighting Malicious Code. Prentice Hall Professional. pp. 37–38. ISBN 9780131014053.
59. Dave Jones. 2001 (December 2001). "Building an e-mail virus detection system for your network. Linux J. 2001, 92, 2-.".
60. editor-in-chief, Béla G. Lipták, (2002). Instrument engineers' handbook (3rd ed.). Boca Raton: CRC Press. p. 874. ISBN 9781439863442. Retrieved September 4, 2015.
61. "Computer Virus Strategies and Detection Methods" (PDF). Retrieved 2 September 2008.
62. Internet Communication. PediaPress. pp. 163–. GGKEY:Y43AS5T4TFD. Retrieved 16 April 2016.
63. Szor, Peter (2005). The Art of Computer Virus Research and Defense. Boston: Addison-Wesley. p. 285. ISBN 0-321-30454-3.
64. Fox-Brewster, Thomas. "Netflix Is Dumping Anti-Virus, Presages Death Of An Industry". Forbes. Retrieved September 4, 2015.
65. "How Anti-Virus Software Works". Stanford University. Retrieved September 4, 2015.
66. "www.sans.org". Retrieved 2016-04-16.
67. Jacobs, Stuart (2015-12-01). Engineering Information Security: The Application of Systems Engineering Concepts to Achieve Information Assurance. John Wiley & Sons. ISBN 9781119104711.
68. Bishop, Matt (2003). Computer Security: Art and Science. Addison-Wesley Professional. p. 620. ISBN 9780201440997.
69. Internet Communication. PediaPress. pp. 165–. GGKEY:Y43AS5T4TFD.
70. John Aycock (19 September 2006). Computer Viruses and Malware. Springer. pp. 35–36. ISBN 978-0-387-34188-0.
71. Kizza, Joseph M. (2009). Guide to Computer Network Security. Springer. p. 341. ISBN 9781848009165.
72. Eilam, Eldad (2011). Reversing: Secrets of Reverse Engineering. John Wiley & Sons. p. 216. ISBN 9781118079768.
73. "Virus Bulletin : Glossary – Polymorphic virus". Virusbtn.com. 2009-10-01. Retrieved 2010-08-27.
74. Perriot, Fredrick; Peter Ferrie; Peter Szor (May 2002). "Striking Similarities" (PDF). Retrieved September 9, 2007.
75. "Virus Bulletin : Glossary — Metamorphic virus". Virusbtn.com. Retrieved 2010-08-27.
76. "Virus Basics". US-CERT.
77. "Virus Notice: Network Associates' AVERT Discovers First Virus That Can Infect JPEG Files, Assigns Low-Profiled Risk". Retrieved 2002-06-13.
78. "Operating system market share". netmarketshare.com. Retrieved 2015-05-16.
79. This is analogous to how genetic diversity in a population decreases the chance of a single disease wiping out a population in biology
80. Raggi, Emilio et al. (2011). Beginning Ubuntu Linux. Apress. p. 148. ISBN 9781430236276.
81. "McAfee discovers first Linux virus" (Press release). McAfee, via Axel Boldt. 5 February 1997.
82. Boldt, Axel (19 January 2000). "Bliss, a Linux 'virus'".
83. "Detailed test reports—(Windows) home user". AV-Test.org.
84. "Detailed test reports — Android mobile devices". AV-Test.org.
85. "Microsoft Security Essentials". Retrieved June 21, 2012.
86. "Malicious Software Removal Tool". Archived from the original on June 21, 2012. Retrieved June 21, 2012.
87. "Windows Defender". Retrieved June 21, 2012.
88. Rubenking, Neil J. (Feb 17, 2012). "The Best Free Antivirus for 2012". pcmag.com.
89. Rubenking, Neil J. (Jan 10, 2013). "The Best Antivirus for 2013". pcmag.com.
90. Rubenking, Neil J. "Secunia Personal Software Inspector 3.0 Review & Rating". PCMag.com. Retrieved 2013-01-19.
91. "10 Step Guide to Protect Against Viruses". GrnLight.net. Retrieved 23 May 2014.
92. "Google Safe Browsing".
93. "Report malicious software (URL) to Google".
94. Zhang, Yu et al. (2008). "A Novel Immune Based Approach For Detection of Windows PE Virus". In Tang, Changjie et al. Advanced Data Mining and Applications: 4th International Conference, ADMA 2008, Chengdu, China, October 8-10, 2008, Proceedings. Springer. p. 250. ISBN 9783540881919.
95. "Good Security Habits | US-CERT". Retrieved 2016-04-16.
96. "W32.Gammima.AG". Symantec. Retrieved 2014-07-17.
97. Category: Computer Articles. "Viruses! In! Space!". GrnLight.net. Retrieved 2014-07-17.
98. "VirusTotal.com (a subsidiary of Google)".
99. "VirScan.org".
100. Rubenking, Neil J. "The Best Free Antivirus for 2014". pcmag.com.
101. "Microsoft Safety Scanner".
102. "Virus removal -Help". Retrieved 2015-01-31.
103. "W32.Gammima.AG Removal — Removing Help". Symantec. 2007-08-27. Retrieved 2014-07-17.
104. "support.microsoft.com". Retrieved 2016-04-16.
105. "www.us-cert.gov" (PDF). Retrieved 2016-04-16.
106. David Kim; Michael G. Solomon (17 November 2010). Fundamentals of Information Systems Security. Jones & Bartlett Publishers. pp. 360–. ISBN 978-1-4496-7164-8.
107. "1980s – Securelist – Information about Viruses, Hackers and Spam". Retrieved 2016-04-16.
108. Internet Communication. PediaPress. pp. 160–. GGKEY:Y43AS5T4TFD.
109. "What is a Computer Virus?". Actlab.utexas.edu. 1996-03-31. Retrieved 2010-08-27.
110. Realtimepublishers.com (1 January 2005). The Definitive Guide to Controlling Malware, Spyware, Phishing, and Spam. Realtimepublishers.com. pp. 48–. ISBN 978-1-931491-44-0.
111. Eli B. Cohen (2011). Navigating Information Challenges. Informing Science. pp. 27–. ISBN 978-1-932886-47-4.
112. Vesselin Bontchev. "Macro Virus Identification Problems". FRISK Software International. Archived from the original on 2012-08-05.
113. "Facebook 'photo virus' spreads via email.". Retrieved 2014-04-28.
114. Berend-Jan Wever. "XSS bug in hotmail login page". Retrieved 2014-04-07.
115. Wade Alcorn. "The Cross-site Scripting Virus". bindshell.net. Retrieved 2015-10-13.

Computer Worm, References

1. Barwise, Mike. "What is an internet worm?". BBC. Retrieved 9 September 2010.
2. Brunner, John (1975). The Shockwave Rider. New York: Ballantine Books. ISBN 0-06-010559-3.
3. "The Submarine".
4. "Security of the Internet". CERT/CC.
5. "Phage mailing list". securitydigest.org.
6. Dressler, J. (2007). "United States v. Morris". Cases and Materials on Criminal Law. St. Paul, MN: Thomson/West. ISBN 978-0-314-17719-3.
7. Ray, Tiernan (February 18, 2004). "Business & Technology: E-mail viruses blamed as spam rises sharply". The Seattle Times.
8. McWilliams, Brian (October 9, 2003). "Cloaking Device Made for Spammers". Wired.
9. "Mydoom Internet worm likely from Russia, linked to spam mail: security firm". www.channelnewsasia.com. 31 January 2004. Archived from the original on 2006-02-19.
10. "Uncovered: Trojans as Spam Robots". Hiese online. 2004-02-21. Archived from the original on 2009-05-28. Retrieved 2012-11-02.
11. "Hacker threats to bookies probed". BBC News. February 23, 2004.
12. "USN list". Ubuntu. Retrieved 2012-06-10.
13. Threat Description Email-Worm
14. Threat Description Email-Worm: VBS/LoveLetter
15. Sellke, S. H.; Shroff, N. B.; Bagchi, S. (2008). "Modeling and Automated Containment of Worms". IEEE Transactions on Dependable and Secure Computing. **5** (2): 71–86. doi:10.1109/tdsc.2007.70230. Archived from the original on 25 May 2015.
16. "A New Way to Protect Computer Networks from Internet Worms". Newswise. Retrieved July 5, 2011.
17. Moskovitch R., Elovici Y., Rokach L. (2008), "Detection of unknown computer worms based on behavioral classification of the host", *Computational Statistics and Data Analysis*, 52(9):4544–4566, doi:10.1016/j.csda.2008.01.028
18. "Computer Worm Information and Removal Steps". Veracode. Retrieved 2015-04-04.
19. "Virus alert about the Nachi worm". Microsoft.
20. Al-Salloum, Z. S.; Wolthusen, S. D. (2010). "A link-layer-based self-replicating vulnerability discovery agent". The IEEE symposium on Computers and Communications. p. 704. ISBN 978-1-4244-7754-8. doi:10.1109/ISCC.2010.5546723.

Trojan Hourse, References

- Carnegie Mellon University (1999): "CERT Advisory CA-1999-02 Trojan Horses", ŸЦ

1. Landwehr, C. E; A. R Bull; J. P McDermott; W. S Choi (1993). A taxonomy of computer program security flaws, with examples. DTIC Document. Retrieved 2012-04-05.
2. "Trojan Horse Definition". Retrieved 2012-04-05.
3. Data theft == "Trojan horse" Check |url= value (help). Webopedia. Retrieved 2012-04-05.
4. "What is Trojan horse? – Definition from Whatis.com". Retrieved 2012-04-05.
5. "Trojan Horse: [coined By MIT-hacker-turned-NSA-spook Dan Edwards] N.". Retrieved 2012-04-05.
6. "What is the difference between viruses, worms, and Trojans?". Symantec Corporation. Retrieved 2009-01-10.
7. "VIRUS-L/comp.virus Frequently Asked Questions (FAQ) v2.00 (Question B3: What is a Trojan Horse?)". 9 October 1995. Retrieved 2012-09-13.
8. Jamie Crapanzano (2003): "Deconstructing SubSeven, the Trojan Horse of Choice", SANS Institute, Retrieved on 2009-06-11
9. Vincentas (11 July 2013). "Trojan Horse in SpyWareLoop.com". Spyware Loop. Retrieved 28 July 2013.
10. Basil Cupa, Trojan Horse Resurrected: On the Legality of the Use of Government Spyware (Govware), LISS 2013, pp. 419–428
11. "Dokument nicht gefunden!". Federal Department of Justice and Police. Archived from the original on May 6, 2013.
12. "Swiss coder publicises government spy Trojan – Techworld.com". News.techworld.com. Retrieved 2014-01-26.
13. BitDefender.com Malware and Spam Survey
14. Datta, Ganesh. "What are Trojans?". SecurAid.
15. "Mega-Panzer".
16. "Mini-Panzer".
17. "Trojanized adware family abuses accessibility service to install whatever apps it wants - Lookout Blog".
18. "Shedun trojan adware is hitting the Android Accessibility Service - TheINQUIRER".
19. "Lookout discovers new trojanized adware; 20K popular apps caught in the crossfire - Lookout Blog".
20. "Shuanet, ShiftyBug and Shedun malware could auto-root your Android". 5 November 2015.
21. Times, Tech (9 November 2015). "New Family Of Android Malware Virtually Impossible To Remove: Say Hello To Shedun, Shuanet And ShiftyBug".
22. "Android adware can install itself even when users explicitly reject it".

Root Kit, Notes

1. The process name of Sysinternals RootkitRevealer was targeted by malware; in an attempt to counter this countermeasure, the tool now uses a randomly generated process name.
2. In theory, a sufficiently sophisticated kernel-level rootkit could subvert read operations against raw filesystem data structures as well, so that they match the results returned by APIs.

Root Kit, References

1. "Rootkits, Part 1 of 3: The Growing Threat" (PDF). McAfee. 2006-04-17. Archived from the original (PDF) on 2006-08-23.
2. http://www.technibble.com/how-to-remove-a-rootkit-from-a-windows-system/
3. "Windows Rootkit Overview" (PDF). Symantec. 2006-03-26. Retrieved 2010-08-17.
4. Sparks, Sherri; Butler, Jamie (2005-08-01). "Raising The Bar For Windows Rootkit Detection". Phrack. **0xb** (0x3d).
5. Myers, Michael; Youndt, Stephen (2007-08-07). "An Introduction to Hardware-Assisted Virtual Machine (HVM) Rootkits". Crucial Security. CiteSeerX: 10.1.1.90.8832.
6. Andrew Hay; Daniel Cid; Rory Bray (2008). OSSEC Host-Based Intrusion Detection Guide. Syngress. p. 276. ISBN 1-59749-240-X.
7. Thompson, Ken (August 1984). "Reflections on Trusting Trust" (PDF). Communications of the ACM. **27** (8): 761. doi:10.1145/358198.358210.
8. Greg Hoglund; James Butler (2006). Rootkits: Subverting the Windows kernel. Addison-Wesley. p. 4. ISBN 0-321-29431-9.
9. Dai Zovi, Dino (2009-07-26). Advanced Mac OS X Rootkits (PDF). Blackhat. Endgame Systems. Retrieved 2010-11-23.
10. "Stuxnet Introduces the First Known Rootkit for Industrial Control Systems". Symantec. 2010-08-06. Retrieved 2010-12-04.
11. "Spyware Detail: XCP.Sony.Rootkit". Computer Associates. 2005-11-05. Archived from the original on 2010-08-18. Retrieved 2010-08-19.
12. Russinovich, Mark (2005-10-31). "Sony, Rootkits and Digital Rights Management Gone Too Far". TechNet Blogs. Microsoft. Retrieved 2010-08-16.
13. "Sony's long-term rootkit CD woes". BBC News. 2005-11-21. Retrieved 2008-09-15.
14. Felton, Ed (2005-11-15). "Sony's Web-Based Uninstaller Opens a Big Security Hole; Sony to Recall Discs".
15. Knight, Will (2005-11-11). "Sony BMG sued over cloaking software on music CD". New Scientist. Sutton, UK: Reed Business Information. Retrieved 2010-11-21.
16. Kyriakidou, Dina (March 2, 2006). ""Greek Watergate" Scandal Sends Political Shockwaves". Reuters. Retrieved 2007-11-24.[dead link]
17. Vassilis Prevelakis; Diomidis Spinellis (July 2007). "The Athens Affair".
18. Russinovich, Mark (June 2005). "Unearthing Root Kits". Windows IT Pro. Retrieved 2010-12-16.
19. "World of Warcraft Hackers Using Sony BMG Rootkit". The Register. 2005-11-04. Retrieved 2010-08-23.
20. Steve Hanna (September 2007). "Using Rootkit Technology for Honeypot-Based Malware Detection" (PDF). CCEID Meeting.
21. Russinovich, Mark (6 February 2006). "Using Rootkits to Defeat Digital Rights Management". Winternals. SysInternals. Archived from the original on 14 August 2006. Retrieved 2006-08-13.
22. Ortega, Alfredo; Sacco, Anibal (2009-07-24). Deactivate the Rootkit: Attacks on BIOS anti-theft technologies (PDF). Black Hat USA 2009 (PDF). Boston, MA: Core Security Technologies. Retrieved 2014-06-12.
23. Kleissner, Peter (2009-09-02). "Stoned Bootkit: The Rise of MBR Rootkits & Bootkits in the Wild" (PDF). Retrieved 2010-11-23.
24. Anson, Steve; Bunting, Steve (2007). Mastering Windows Network Forensics and Investigation. John Wiley and Sons. pp. 73–74. ISBN 0-470-09762-0.
25. "Rootkits Part 2: A Technical Primer" (PDF). McAfee. 2007-04-03. Archived from the original (PDF) on 2008-12-05. Retrieved 2010-08-17.
26. Kdm. "NTIllusion: A portable Win32 userland rootkit". Phrack. **62** (12).
27. "Understanding Anti-Malware Technologies" (PDF). Microsoft. 2007-02-21. Retrieved 2010-08-17.
28. Hoglund, Greg (1999-09-09). "A *REAL* NT Rootkit, Patching the NT Kernel". Phrack. **9** (55). Retrieved 2010-11-21.
29. Shevchenko, Alisa (2008-09-01). "Rootkit Evolution". Help Net Security. Help Net Security.
30. Chuvakin, Anton (2003-02-02). An Overview of Unix Rootkits (PDF) (Report). Chantilly, Virginia: iDEFENSE. Retrieved 2010-11-21.
31. Butler, James; Sparks, Sherri (2005-11-16). "Windows Rootkits of 2005, Part Two". Symantec Connect. Symantec. Retrieved 2010-11-13.
32. Butler, James; Sparks, Sherri (2005-11-03). "Windows Rootkits of 2005, Part One". Symantec Connect. Symantec. Retrieved 2010-11-12.
33. Burdach, Mariusz (2004-11-17). "Detecting Rootkits And Kernel-level Compromises In Linux". Symantec. Retrieved 2010-11-23.
34. Marco Giuliani (11 April 2011). "ZeroAccess – An Advanced Kernel Mode Rootkit" (PDF). Webroot Software. Retrieved 10 August 2011.
35. "Driver Signing Requirements for Windows". Microsoft. Retrieved 2008-07-06.
36. Soeder, Derek; Permeh, Ryan (2007-05-09). "Bootroot". eEye Digital Security. Archived from the original on 2013-08-17. Retrieved 2010-11-23.
37. Schneier, Bruce (2009-10-23). "'Evil Maid' Attacks on Encrypted Hard Drives". Retrieved 2009-11-07.
38. Kumar, Nitin; Kumar, Vipin (2007). Vbootkit: Compromising Windows Vista Security (PDF). Black Hat Europe 2007.
39. "BOOT KIT: Custom boot sector based Windows 2000/XP/2003 Subversion". NVlabs. 2007-02-04. Archived from the original on June 10, 2010. Retrieved 2010-11-21.
40. Kleissner, Peter (2009-10-19). "Stoned Bootkit". Peter Kleissner. Retrieved 2009-11-07.[self-published source?]
41. Goodin, Dan (2010-11-16). "World's Most Advanced Rootkit Penetrates 64-bit Windows". The Register. Retrieved 2010-11-22.
42. Peter Kleissner, "The Rise of MBR Rootkits And Bootkits in the Wild", Hacking at Random (2009) - text; slides
43. Windows Loader - Software Informer. This is the loader application that's used by millions of people worldwide
44. Microsoft tightens grip on OEM Windows 8 licensing
45. King, Samuel T.; Chen, Peter M.; Wang, Yi-Min; Verbowski, Chad; Wang, Helen J.; Lorch, Jacob R. (2006-04-03). International Business Machines (ed.), ed. SubVirt: Implementing malware with virtual machines (PDF). 2006 IEEE Symposium on Security and Privacy. Institute of Electrical and Electronics Engineers. ISBN 0-7695-2574-1. doi:10.1109/SP.2006.38. Retrieved 2008-09-15.
46. Wang, Zhi; Jiang, Xuxian; Cui, Weidong; Ning, Peng (2009-08-11). "Countering Kernel Rootkits with Lightweight Hook Protection" (PDF). In Al-Shaer, Ehab (General Chair). Proceedings of the 16th ACM Conference on Computer and Communications Security. CCS 2009: 16th ACM Conference on Computer and Communications Security. Jha, Somesh; Keromytis, Angelos D. (Program Chairs). New York: ACM New York. ISBN 978-1-60558-894-0. doi:10.1145/1653662.1653728. Retrieved 2009-11-11.
47. https://msdn.microsoft.com/en-us/library/dn986865(v=vs.85).aspx
48. Delugré, Guillaume (2010-11-21). Reversing the Broacom NetExtreme's Firmware (PDF). hack.lu. Sogeti. Archived from the original (PDF) on 2012-04-25. Retrieved 2010-11-25.
49. http://blog.trendmicro.com/trendlabs-security-intelligence/hacking-team-uses-uefi-bios-rootkit-to-keep-rcs-9-agent-in-target-systems/
50. Heasman, John (2006-01-25). Implementing and Detecting an ACPI BIOS Rootkit (PDF). Black Hat Federal 2006. NGS Consulting. Retrieved 2010-11-21.
51. Heasman, John (2006-11-15). "Implementing and Detecting a PCI Rootkit" (PDF). Next Generation Security Software. CiteSeerX: 10.1.1.89.7305. Retrieved 2010-11-13.
52. Modine, Austin (2008-10-10). "Organized crime tampers with European card swipe devices: Customer data beamed overseas". The Register. Situation Publishing. Retrieved 2008-10-13.
53. Sacco, Anibal; Ortéga, Alfredo (2009). Persistent BIOS infection (PDF). CanSecWest 2009. Core Security Technologies. Retrieved 2010-11-21.
54. Goodin, Dan (2009-03-24). "Newfangled rootkits survive hard disk wiping". The Register. Situation Publishing. Retrieved 2009-03-25.
55. Sacco, Anibal; Ortéga, Alfredo (2009-06-01). "Persistent BIOS Infection: The Early Bird Catches the Worm". Phrack. **66** (7). Retrieved 2010-11-13.
56. Ric Vieler (2007). Professional Rootkits. John Wiley & Sons. p. 244. ISBN 9780470149546.
57. Matrosov, Aleksandr; Rodionov, Eugene (2010-06-25). "TDL3: The Rootkit of All Evil?" (PDF). Moscow: ESET. p. 3. Retrieved 2010-08-17.
58. Matrosov, Aleksandr; Rodionov, Eugene (2011-06-27). "The Evolution of TDL: Conquering x64" (PDF). ESET. Retrieved 2011-08-08.
59. Brumley, David (1999-11-16). "Invisible Intruders: rootkits in practice". USENIX. USENIX.
60. Davis, Michael A.; Bodmer, Sean; LeMasters, Aaron (2009-09-03). "Chapter 10: Rootkit Detection" (PDF). Hacking Exposed Malware & Rootkits: Malware & rootkits security secrets & solutions (PDF). New York: McGraw Hill Professional. ISBN 978-0-07-159118-8. Retrieved 2010-08-14.
61. Trlokom (2006-07-05). "Defeating Rootkits and Keyloggers" (PDF). Trlokom. Retrieved 2010-08-17.
62. Dai Zovi, Dino (2011). "Kernel Rootkits". Archived from the original on September 10, 2012. Retrieved 13 Sep 2012.
63. "Zeppoo". SourceForge. 18 July 2009. Retrieved 8 August 2011.
64. Cogswell, Bryce; Russinovich, Mark (2006-11-01). "RootkitRevealer v1.71". Microsoft. Retrieved 2010-11-13.
65. "Sophos Anti-Rootkit". Sophos. Retrieved 8 August 2011.
66. "BlackLight". F-Secure. Retrieved 8 August 2011.
67. "Radix Anti-Rootkit". usec.at. Retrieved 8 August 2011.
68. "GMER". Retrieved 8 August 2011.
69. Harriman, Josh (2007-10-19). "A Testing Methodology for Rootkit Removal Effectiveness" (PDF). Dublin, Ireland: Symantec Security Response. Retrieved 2010-08-17.
70. Cuibotariu, Mircea (2010-02-12). "Tidserv and MS10-015". Symantec. Retrieved 2010-08-19.
71. "Restart Issues After Installing MS10-015". Microsoft. 2010-02-11. Retrieved 2010-10-05.
72. "Strider GhostBuster Rootkit Detection". Microsoft Research. 2010-01-28. Retrieved 2010-08-14.
73. "Signing and Checking Code with Authenticode". Microsoft. Retrieved 2008-09-15.
74. "Stopping Rootkits at the Network Edge" (PDF). Beaverton, Oregon: Trusted Computing Group. January 2007. Retrieved 2008-07-11.
75. "TCG PC Specific Implementation Specification, Version 1.1" (PDF). Trusted Computing Group. 2003-08-18. Retrieved 2010-11-22.
76. "How to generate a complete crash dump file or a kernel crash dump file by using an NMI on a Windows-based system". Microsoft. Retrieved 2010-11-13.
77. Seshadri, Arvind; et al. (2005). "Pioneer: Verifying Code Integrity and Enforcing Untampered Code Execution on Legacy Systems". Carnegie Mellon University.
78. Dillard, Kurt (2005-08-03). "Rootkit battle: Rootkit Revealer vs. Hacker Defender".
79. "The Microsoft Windows Malicious Software Removal Tool helps remove specific, prevalent malicious software from computers that are running Windows 7, Windows Vista, Windows Server 2003, Windows Server 2008, or Windows XP". Microsoft. 2010-09-14.
80. Hultquist, Steve (2007-04-30). "Rootkits: The next big enterprise threat?". InfoWorld. IDG. Retrieved 2010-11-21.
81. "Security Watch: Rootkits for fun and profit". CNET Reviews. 2007-01-19. Archived from the original on 2012-10-08. Retrieved 2009-04-07.
82. Bort, Julie (2007-09-29). "Six ways to fight back against botnets". PCWorld. San Francisco: PCWorld Communications. Retrieved 2009-04-07.
83. Hoang, Mimi (2006-11-02). "Handling Today's Tough Security Threats: Rootkits". Symantec Connect. Symantec. Retrieved 2010-11-21.
84. Danseglio, Mike; Bailey, Tony (2005-10-06). "Rootkits: The Obscure Hacker Attack". Microsoft.
85. Messmer, Ellen (2006-08-26). "Experts Divided Over Rootkit Detection and Removal". NetworkWorld.com. Framingham, Mass.: IDG. Retrieved 2010-08-15.
86. Stevenson, Larry; Altholz, Nancy (2007). Rootkits for Dummies. John Wiley and Sons Ltd. p. 175. ISBN 0-471-91710-9.
87. Skoudis, Ed; Zeltser, Lenny (2004). Malware: Fighting Malicious Code. Prentice Hall PTR. p. 335. ISBN 0-13-101405-6.
88. Hannel, Jeromey (2003-01-23). "Linux RootKits For Beginners - From Prevention to Removal". SANS Institute. Archived from the original (PDF) on October 24, 2010. Retrieved 2010-11-22.

Man-in-the-middle Attack, References

1. Tanmay Patange (November 10, 2013). "How to defend yourself against MITM or Man-in-the-middle attack".
2. Callegati, Franco; Cerroni, Walter; Ramilli, Marco (2009). "IEEE Xplore - Man-in-the-Middle Attack to the HTTPS Protocol". ieeexplore.ieee.org: 78–81. Retrieved 13 April 2016.
3. MiTM on RSA public key encryption
4. How Encryption Works
5. Public-key cryptography
6. Merkle, Ralph C (April 1978). "Secure Communications Over Insecure Channels". Communications of the ACM. **21** (4): 294–299. doi:10.1145/359460.359473. Received August, 1975; revised September 1977
7. Heinrich, Stuart (2013). "Public Key Infrastructure based on Authentication of Media Attestments". arXiv:1311.7182v1 .
8. Aziz, Benjamin; Hamilton, Geoff (2009). "Detecting man-in-the-middle attacks by precise timing.". 2009 Third International Conference on Emerging Security Information, Systems and Technologies: 81–86. Retrieved 2017-02-25.
9. "5. Unconditionally secure authentication". liu.se.

10.   "Network Forensic Analysis of SSL MITM Attacks". NETRESEC Network Security Blog. Retrieved March 27, 2011.
11.   Leyden, John (2003-11-07). "Help! my Belkin router is spamming me". The Register.
12.   Meyer, David (10 January 2013). "Nokia: Yes, we decrypt your HTTPS data, but don't worry about it". Gigaom, Inc. Retrieved 13 June 2014.
13.   "NSA disguised itself as Google to spy, say reports". CNET. 12 Sep 2013. Retrieved 15 Sep 2013.

Denial-of-service Attack, References

1.   "Understanding Denial-of-Service Attacks". US-CERT. 6 February 2013. Retrieved 26 May 2016.
2.   Prince, Matthew (25 April 2016). "Empty DDoS Threats: Meet the Armada Collective". CloudFlare. Retrieved 18 May 2016.
3.   "Brand.com President Mike Zammuto Reveals Blackmail Attempt". 5 March 2014. Archived from the original on 11 March 2014.
4.   "Brand.com's Mike Zammuto Discusses Meetup.com Extortion". 5 March 2014. Archived from the original on 13 May 2014.
5.   "The Philosophy of Anonymous". Radicalphilosophy.com. 2010-12-17. Retrieved 2013-09-10.
6.   Smith, Steve. "5 Famous Botnets that held the internet hostage". tqaweekly. Retrieved November 20, 2014.
7.   Taghavi Zargar, Saman (November 2013). "A Survey of Defense Mechanisms Against Distributed Denial of Service (DDoS) Flooding Attacks" (PDF). IEEE COMMUNICATIONS SURVEYS & TUTORIALS. pp. 2046–2069. Retrieved 2014-03-07.
8.   Goodin, Dan (28 September 2016). "Record-breaking DDoS reportedly delivered by >145k hacked cameras". Ars Technica. Archived from the original on 2 October 2016.
9.   Khandelwal, Swati (26 September 2016). "World's largest 1 Tbps DDoS Attack launched from 152,000 hacked Smart Devices". The Hacker News. Archived from the original on 30 September 2016.
10.   Lee, Newton (2013). Counterterrorism and Cybersecurity: Total Information Awareness. Springer. ISBN 9781461472056.
11.   "Layer Seven DDoS Attacks". Infosec Institute.
12.   "Gartner Says 25 Percent of Distributed Denial of Services Attacks in 2013 Will Be Application - Based". Gartner. 21 February 2013. Retrieved 28 January 2014.
13.   Ginovsky, John (27 January 2014). "What you should know about worsening DDoS attacks". ABA Banking Journal. Retrieved 28 January 2014.
14.   "Q4 2014 State of the Internet - Security Report: Numbers - The Akamai Blog". blogs.akamai.com.
15.   Higgins, Kelly Jackson (17 October 2013). "DDoS Attack Used 'Headless' Browser In 150-Hour Siege". Dark Reading. InformationWeek. Archived from the original on January 22, 2014. Retrieved 28 January 2014.
16.   Raghavan, S.V. (2011). An Investigation into the Detection and Mitigation of Denial of Service (DoS) Attacks. Springer. ISBN 9788132202776.
17.   Kiyuna and Conyers (2015). Cyberwarfare Sourcebook. ISBN 1329063945.
18.   Gold, Steve (21 August 2014). "Video games company hit by 38-day DDoS attack". SC Magazine UK. Retrieved 4 February 2016.
19.   Krebs, Brian (August 15, 2015). "Stress-Testing the Booter Services, Financially". Krebs on Security. Retrieved 2016-09-09.
20.   McDowell, Mindi (November 4, 2009). "Cyber Security Tip ST04-015 - Understanding Denial-of-Service Attacks". United States Computer Emergency Readiness Team. Archived from the original on 2013-11-04. Retrieved December 11, 2013.
21.   Dittrich, David (December 31, 1999). "The "stacheldraht" distributed denial of service attack tool". University of Washington. Retrieved 2013-12-11.
22.   Glenn Greenwald (2014-07-15). "HACKING ONLINE POLLS AND OTHER WAYS BRITISH SPIES SEEK TO CONTROL THE INTERNET". The Intercept_. Retrieved 2015-12-25.
23.   "Amazon CloudWatch". Amazon Web Services, Inc.
24.   Encyclopaedia Of Information Technology. Atlantic Publishers & Distributors. 2007. p. 397. ISBN 81-269-0752-5.
25.   Schwabach, Aaron (2006). Internet and the Law. ABC-CLIO. p. 325. ISBN 1-85109-731-7.
26.   Lu, Xicheng; Wei Zhao (2005). Networking and Mobile Computing. Birkhäuser. p. 424. ISBN 3-540-28102-9.
27.   "Has Your Website Been Bitten By a Zombie?". Cloudbric. 3 August 2015. Retrieved 15 September 2015.
28.   Boyle, Phillip (2000). "SANS Institute – Intrusion Detection FAQ: Distributed Denial of Service Attack Tools: n/a". SANS Institute. Retrieved 2008-05-02.
29.   Leyden, John (2004-09-23). "US credit card firm fights DDoS attack". The Register. Retrieved 2011-12-02.
30.   Swati Khandelwal (23 October 2015). "Hacking CCTV Cameras to Launch DDoS Attacks". The Hacker News.
31.   Zeifman, Igal; Gayer, Ofer; Wilder, Or (21 October 2015). "CCTV DDoS Botnet In Our Own Back Yard". incapsula.com.
32.   "Who's Behind DDoS Attacks and How Can You Protect Your Website?". Cloudbric. 10 September 2015. Retrieved 15 September 2015.
33.   Solon, Olivia (9 September 2015). "Cyber-Extortionists Targeting the Financial Sector Are Demanding Bitcoin Ransoms". Bloomberg. Retrieved 15 September 2015.
34.   Greenberg, Adam (14 September 2015). "Akamai warns of increased activity from DDoS extortion group". SC Magazine. Retrieved 15 September 2015.
35.   "OWASP Plan - Strawman - Layer_7_DDOS.pdf" (PDF). Open Web Application Security Project. 18 March 2014. Retrieved 18 March 2014.
36.   "Types of DDoS Attacks". Distributed Denial of Service Attacks(DDoS) Resources, Pervasive Technology Labs at Indiana University. Advanced Networking Management Lab (ANML). December 3, 2009. Archived from the original on 2010-09-14. Retrieved December 11, 2013.
37.   Paul Sop (May 2007). "Prolexic Distributed Denial of Service Attack Alert". Prolexic Technologies Inc. Prolexic Technologies Inc. Archived from the original on 2007-08-03. Retrieved 2007-08-22.
38.   Robert Lemos (May 2007). "Peer-to-peer networks co-opted for DOS attacks". SecurityFocus. Retrieved 2007-08-22.
39.   Fredrik Ullner (May 2007). "Denying distributed attacks". DC++: Just These Guys, Ya Know?. Retrieved 2007-08-22.
40.   Leyden, John (2008-05-21). "Phlashing attack thrashes embedded systems". The Register. Retrieved 2009-03-07.
41.   Jackson Higgins, Kelly (May 19, 2008). "Permanent Denial-of-Service Attack Sabotages Hardware". Dark Reading. Archived from the original on December 8, 2008.
42.   "EUSecWest Applied Security Conference: London, U.K.". EUSecWest. 2008. Archived from the original on 2009-02-01.
43.   Rossow, Christian (February 2014). "Amplification Hell: Revisiting Network Protocols for DDoS Abuse" (PDF). Internet Society. Retrieved 4 February 2016.
44.   Paxson, Vern (2001). "An Analysis of Using Reflectors for Distributed Denial-of-Service Attacks". ICIR.org.
45.   "Alert (TA14-017A) UDP-based Amplification Attacks". US-CERT. July 8, 2014. Retrieved 2014-07-08.
46.   van Rijswijk-Deij, Roland (2014). "DNSSEC and its potential for DDoS attacks - a comprehensive measurement study". ACM Press.
47.   Adamsky, Florian (2015). "P2P File-Sharing in Hell: Exploiting BitTorrent Vulnerabilities to Launch Distributed Reflective DoS Attacks".
48.   Vaughn, Randal; Evron, Gadi (2006). "DNS Amplification Attacks" (PDF). ISOTF. Archived from the original (PDF) on 2010-12-14.
49.   "Alert (TA13-088A) DNS Amplification Attacks". US-CERT. July 8, 2013. Retrieved 2013-07-17.
50.   Yu Chen; Kai Hwang; Yu-Kwong Kwok (2005). "Filtering of shrew DDoS attacks in frequency domain". The IEEE Conference on Local Computer Networks 30th Anniversary (LCN'05)l. pp. 8 pp. ISBN 0-7695-2421-4. doi:10.1109/LCN.2005.70.
51.   Ben-Porat, U.; Bremler-Barr, A.; Levy, H. (2013-05-01). "Vulnerability of Network Mechanisms to Sophisticated DDoS Attacks". IEEE Transactions on Computers. 62 (5): 1031–1043. ISSN 0018-9340. doi:10.1109/TC.2012.49.
52.   orbitalsatelite. "Slow HTTP Test". SourceForge.
53.   "RFC 4987 - TCP SYN Flooding Attacks and Common Mitigations". Tools.ietf.org. August 2007. Retrieved 2011-12-02.
54.   "CERT Advisory CA-1997-28 IP Denial-of-Service Attacks". CERT. 1998. Retrieved July 18, 2014.
55.   "Windows 7, Vista exposed to 'teardrop attack'". ZDNet. September 8, 2009. Retrieved 2013-12-11.
56.   "Microsoft Security Advisory (975497): Vulnerabilities in SMB Could Allow Remote Code Execution". Microsoft.com. September 8, 2009. Retrieved 2011-12-02.
57.   "FBI — Phony Phone Calls Distract Consumers from Genuine Theft". FBI.gov. 2010-05-11. Retrieved 2013-09-10.
58.   "Internet Crime Complaint Center's (IC3) Scam Alerts January 7, 2013". IC3.gov. 2013-01-07. Retrieved 2013-09-10.
59.   Loukas, G.; Oke, G. (September 2010) [August 2009]. "Protection Against Denial of Service Attacks: A Survey" (PDF). Comput. J. 53 (7): 1020–1037. doi:10.1093/comjnl/bxp078.
60.   Alqahtani, S.; Gamble, R. F. (1 January 2015). "DDoS Attacks in Service Clouds". 2015 48th Hawaii International Conference on System Sciences (HICSS): 5331–5340. doi:10.1109/HICSS.2015.627.
61.   Kousiouris, George (2014). "KEY COMPLETION INDICATORS: minimizing the effect of DoS attacks on elastic Cloud-based applications based on application-level markov chain checkpoints". CLOSER Conference. Retrieved 2015-05-24.
62.   Patrikakis, C.; Masikos, M.; Zouraraki, O. (December 2004). "Distributed Denial of Service Attacks". The Internet Protocol Journal. 7 (4): 13–35.
63.   Abante, Carl (March 2, 2013). "Relationship between Firewalls and Protection against DDoS". Ecommerce Wisdom. Retrieved 2013-05-24. [dubious – discuss]
64.   Froutan, Paul (June 24, 2004). "How to defend against DDoS attacks". Computerworld. Retrieved May 15, 2010.
65.   Suzen, Mehmet. "Some IoS tips for Internet Service (Providers)" (PDF). Archived from the original (PDF) on 2008-09-10.
66.   "DDoS Mitigation via Regional Cleaning Centers (Jan 2004)" (PDF). SprintLabs.com. Sprint ATL Research. Archived from the original (PDF) on 2008-09-21. Retrieved 2011-12-02.
67.   Lunden, Ingrid (December 2, 2013). "Akamai Buys DDoS Prevention Specialist Prolexic For $370M To Ramp Up Security Offerings For Enterprises". TechCrunch. Retrieved September 23, 2014.
68.   Gallagher, Sean. "Biggest DDoS ever aimed at Cloudflare's content delivery network". Ars Technica. Retrieved 18 May 2016.
69.   "Level 3 DDoS Mitigation". level3.com. Retrieved 9 May 2016.
70.   "Defensepipe". radware.com. Retrieved 9 November 2015.
71.   "Clean Pipes DDoS Protection and Mitigation from Arbor Networks & Cisco". ArborNetworks.com. 8 August 2013.
72.   "AT&T Internet Protect Distributed Denial of Service Defense" (PDF). ATT.com (Product brief). 16 October 2012.
73.   "Silverline DDoS Protection service". f5.com. Retrieved 24 March 2015.
74.   "Infrastructure DDos Protection". incapsula.com. Retrieved 10 June 2015.
75.   "DDoS Protection". Neustar.biz. Retrieved 13 November 2014.
76.   "DDoS Protection with Network Agnostic Option". Tatacommunications.com. 7 September 2011.
77.   "VeriSign Rolls Out DDoS Monitoring Service". Darkreading.com. 11 September 2009. Retrieved 2 December 2011.
78.   "Security: Enforcement and Protection". Verizon.com. Retrieved 10 January 2015.
79.   "Verizon Digital Media Services Launches Cloud-Based Web Application Firewall That Increases Defenses Against Cyberattacks". Verizon.com. Retrieved 10 January 2015.
80.   Shiels, Maggie (2009-06-26). "Web slows after Jackson's death". BBC News.
81.   "We're Sorry. Automated Query error". Google Product Forums › Google Search Forum. Google.com. October 20, 2009. Retrieved 2012-02-11.
82.   "YouTube sued by sound-alike site". BBC News. 2006-11-02.
83.   Bill Chappell (12 March 2014). "People Overload Website, Hoping To Help Search For Missing Jet". NPR. Retrieved 4 February 2016.
84.   "Backscatter Analysis (2001)". Animations (video). Cooperative Association for Internet Data Analysis. Retrieved December 11, 2013.
85.   "United States Code: Title 18,1030. Fraud and related activity in connection with computers | Government Printing Office". www.gpo.gov. 2002-10-25. Retrieved 2014-01-15.
86.   "International Action Against DD4BC Cybercriminal Group". EUROPOL. 12 January 2016.
87.   "Computer Misuse Act 1990". legislation.gov.uk — The National Archives, of UK. 10 January 2008.
88.   "Anonymous DDoS Petition: Group Calls On White House To Recognize Distributed Denial Of Service As Protest.". HuffingtonPost.com. 2013-01-12.
89.   "DDOS Attack: crime or virtual sit-in?". RT.com. YouTube.com. October 6, 2011.

COMPTIA
SECURITY+™

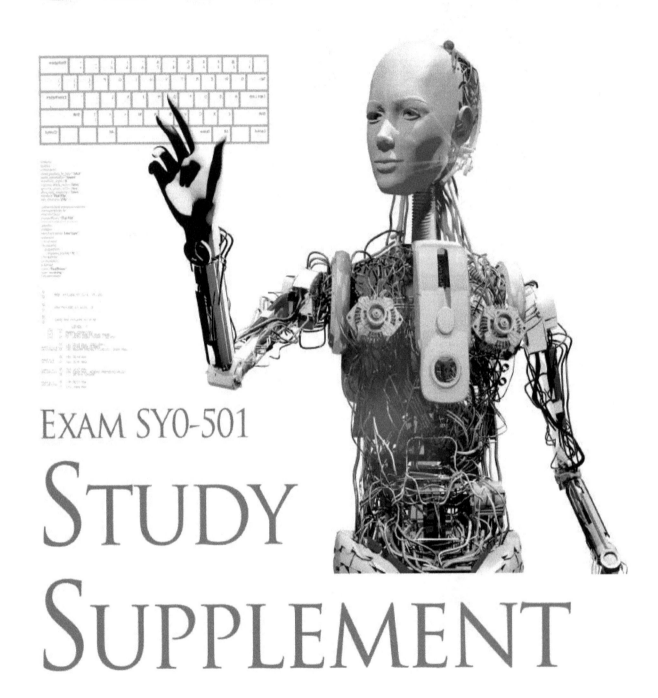

EXAM SY0-501
STUDY
SUPPLEMENT